Other People's Granddads

Petrina Binney

Published by Petrina Binney, 2019.

OTHER PEOPLE'S GRANDDADS

First edition. November 3, 2019.

Written by Petrina Binney.

The profits from this book will be donated to the Royal British Legion's Poppy Appeal. Many thanks for your support.

Foreword

AS A WRITER, OF SORTS, I have spent the greater part of my adult life in a bar. Working or drinking, often both at once. In the ten years I've spent working at my local Royal British Legion Club, I have met some of my favourite people in the world. They have educated me, laughed with me, looked after me. In short, they have become my family.

I know I occupy a strange place in the world. I am neither daughter nor granddaughter. I have never experienced military life. My geographical knowledge is almost non-existent, and there are things I don't know about because they're not in films. I am a thirty-something funny girl: fond of people, not well travelled, far from fit, and usually attached to a pint of Guinness, but as such, I hear stories that the rest of the world doesn't.

I think the best tales come from those who have lived them. And that's what this book is: a collection of stories, as told to me, by the men of the Royal British Legion, covering their experiences of military, police and civilian life, from the 1940s to the present.

Special thanks go out to the men who spent time with me: Ivor, Ted, Fred, Sid, Mike, Keith, Ray and Peter, and to the bar staff who looked after us.

The men you will meet in these pages are among the finest people I have ever known. I hope you enjoy getting to know them as much as I have.

Petrina Binney, November 2019

Ivor

"IT STARTS OFF WHEN I was very young and I was awarded a scholarship to Dunstable Grammar School, which was an old Victorian school, built on the traditions of the public schools of the time. A sort of imitation public school, it was very good, strict discipline, high starched collars, very formal.

"It was the tradition that once you reached the age of twelve (I must have been twelve because it was 1937), you joined the school corps. OTC Officers Training Corps. And, in those days, the uniform was an almost exact copy of the uniform of the '14-'18 war; you had the binding round the legs and that sort of thing, but that uniform was dropped in '39 when the War broke out, of course. I liked the corps. I was Corporal, and then later Sergeant. I suppose I liked bossing people about.

"Then the War broke out, of course, in '39 and the LDV were formed. The LDV were the Local Defence Volunteers, which later become the Home Guard. By that time, I'd become a King's Marksman. At Bisley (Surrey), the brighter, better shots went on a coach with instructors to take part in the national competitions, and the winners became King's Marksmen, which meant you had a star on the shoulder of your uniform. We used .303 rifles. So, on the smaller boys, the rifle was about the same height as the boy.

"Then, of course, the people who showed some interest in military training were pulled out to help train the Home Guard, or the LDV as it was. So, I was there, fifteen/sixteen years old at that time, helping to train fifty-year-old bank managers and such. Must have been difficult, but they all received the training without nastiness, and without being treated with disdain, as it were.

2

"And then about 1941, I suppose, I was granted a Lord Lieutenant's Commission. To become an officer in the forces, you 'd have a King's Commission normally, but a Lord Lieutenant's Commission was a sort of halfway house to that. So I became a Second Lieutenant in the Bedford and Herts; I became connected to them through the Cadet Corps. That was great fun. We did lots of marching all over the countryside, taking cover and building hides. You understand, we were fully expecting, in those days, for the Germans to invade. We were almost certain it was going to happen.

"I came to my eighteenth birthday, and I was called up. At that particular moment in time, I wanted to go into the Light Infantry. Brigadier Charles Foss VC wrote to various people with connections, and the only way I could go into one of the Light Infantry Regiments was to sign on for, I think it was, twelve or fourteen years. And at that age, that seemed like a very long time, so I opted out of that.

"At that point in time, the Army had enough, you could join the Navy, or you could become a Bevin Boy. The Bevin Boys were conscripted to work down the mines. They were desperate for hands down the coal mines. I took the Naval option, renounced my Lord Lieutenant's Commission, and joined the Royal Navy.

"25th October 1943, we were told to report to Butlin's Holiday Camp at Skegness. It was called HMS Royal Arthur. It was a land-based frigate. That was a bit of a shock awakening because you had no idea what was going to happen to you.

"You'd arrive there, by train or whatever other means of transport you had, and that night the whole group that came that day would assemble, and they were nearly all eighteen-year-olds but amongst them, several older people. One of them was a police inspector, one was a bank manager, these were chaps in their top-twenties, early thirties. Butlin's Holiday Camp was surmounted by Nissen huts (prefabricated steel huts, with a semi-cylindrical skin of corrugated steel, used extensively during the War). What a week! One designated wash-room, and a row of about ten wash-hand basins in a row. With no plugs.

"There, in Skegness, we were sorted out and given jobs. Everybody with a grammar school education was assumed to be in the top-flight of intelligence and ability. That wasn't necessarily the case, however, all those top-flight people they put into radar, which was something absolutely new. Nobody quite knew what it was. And we were to be trained as radar mechanics. If there was anything *less* suited to me, I can't really think what. I would have done well in the Seaman Branch as an officer, I'm sure, but I had no mechanical ability. It was important because your radar mechanic would be called on at the most desperate times, you could be in the middle of a battle. However, I certainly gave it my best and I laboured on, but I was never a good radar mechanic, I have to admit that.

"I could cope with the maintaining of the ordinary sets. Amongst radar sets were gunnery sets: great, huge things with valves the size of light bulbs, but the diodes of the old gunnery sets were housed in a large room, and I could manage those.

"Having been sorted out into various classes, time went by, and you did your basic training which was bread and butter to me, because I was used to it from the Cadet Corps. So it was no problem. Then we had to do various courses. Those of us who were considered fit to become radar mechanics had to take a six-month course in physics at the equivalent of university, at the North London Polytechnic. So I was being put into physics and chemistry. I'd resigned my commission, so I'd stopped being Second Lieutenant, so I was the lowest of the low.

"Every month, we'd have a strict written test, a big examination, they showed no mercy on that. Those that failed went straight on the bus, and they went to King Alfred... to be officers in the Seaman Branch. If

I'd had any sense, I should have failed an exam to get to where I wanted to be.

"However, I survived the War. That was important.

"Finally, I'd passed all the exams. I didn't think I was a good mechanic but I knew all about it; problem-solving wasn't so easy. If the call came through that there was a fault somewhere, and I was to track it down and mend it, that was the job, it would have to be a fairly simple fault for me to find it.

"So, after the various stages of training, I qualified as a radar mechanic and became a leading hand; this meant you had an anchor on your shoulder. You had to become a leading hand because you had to command the other operators, so you had to have some sort of rank. Like being a Lance Corporal, I suppose, in the Army.

"And all the while I was on this course, we were very close to the Sadler's Wells Theatre (where the ballet used to take place, near The Angel/Islington, we walked around there in Johns Street), all the time we were there, I and the rest of the irks were living in a very old house, which was divided into two large dormitories.

"In one half were the Naval officers, and in the other half were Irish labourers who were working on some project or other. Well, it was the very height of the bombing. We were on the top floor, just under the eaves of this big old place, I think it was four or five storeys, in Long Lane, top of the Old Kent Road. Every night, you could hear pattering on the roof, just above your head; it was shrapnel from the anti-aircraft guns. One night, a fish-canning factory, just behind us, was hit. There was quite a lot of fallout from that.

"However, we survived. In the evening, after supper, we'd walk round the corner to the Bricklayer's Arms, a very famous pub, and we were all dressed in bell-bottoms. You couldn't buy yourself a drink there because the whole place was full of old ladies. Nobody was expecting anything, but they all wanted to buy you a drink, which was rather nice. We'd go the whole length of the Old Kent Road, from the Bricklayer's Arms to Pepys' Hill (which was called Peppy's Hill Park) where you would probably have assignations with young ladies behind the static water tanks. That's not really part of the story.

"After this six month course, we passed out; we changed out of our bell-bottomed sailor-boy suits, and became NCOs (Non-Commissioned Officers) in the Navy. And, of course, the next thing was drafting. So we were sent down to Portsmouth Barracks, where the drafting jonty – a jonty is like a Sergeant Major in charge of discipline in the Navy, he'd be a huge, great officer – would assign you to some position. At that time, you were either for the Mediterranean or the Russian convoys. I knew that it was physically impossible for me to sustain the cold, we'd be frozen up completely in the Russian convoy. However, I was lucky, and I was sent to the Med.

"I was packed off with, I think, three others. We were very, very junior but we joined the mechanics in charge of radar with the Mediterranean fleet.

"We eventually got to our resting place, which was an old cargo liner called HMS Blenheim, which was moored in harbour at Alexandria. It was an accommodation ship, but it was fully-equipped with workshops. Every day, ships passing through would be calling in at Alexandria, and at that time, a very large number of new gadgets were coming out and being fitted to the ships before they went through, and disappeared to the east.

"Our part was controlled by a big Yorkshireman, a Lieutenant. He was hated by everybody. He bullied everyone. Fortunately, I can't remember his name now. Every day we'd be assigned, one of us senior, another junior, to go off to some ship in the harbour which had some kind of problem, and we were to go and solve the problem, and make it right.

"For some reason, I think it was because it was against my will, the Lieutenant Yorkshireman put me forward to play football for the division when I wasn't very good at football. I was used to rugby, but he decided he'd have rid of me through football. He tried to get me posted to a fleet-class destroyer that was coming through on its way to the Japanese War. I later learned that the only person to be killed aboard that ship was the radar mechanic.

"So that worsened my relationship with this Lieutenant whatever-his-name-was. So, he had another go at getting rid of me, and a job came up with the Greek Navy. What happened with the Greek Navy, the Germans pinched all the ships, so they were a Navy with no fleet but they had several hundred good sailors, all distributed around the islands of the Aegean, where they lived. So the Royal Navy gave them six destroyers, to start with, to be crewed by these distributed sailors, but in order to work with the Royal Navy, they had to have liaison staff.

"The first shore leave you got, for everybody, nineteen years old, was terribly exciting. We were kids: we just wanted to know all about women, life. So the first time we went ashore, we went to visit Number 7, Sista Street, which was a naval brothel. It was an official one. That was a real experience. When you're that young, you want to know all about life. And it made me feel sick. It was around a six storey building, and once you got off the ground floor, you moved up from landing to landing to landing, each of which had numbers of girls on them."

<Me: Did you ever lose your heart to any of them?>

"Oh dear me, no. I never went back there.

"But we had plenty of time ashore. The Salvation Army was there, they were wonderful. They ran classes in the evenings. As did Toc H. Toc H was founded to look after the welfare of soldiers and sailors. Both the Salvation Army and Toc H ran these classes to learn Greek.

"We used to, on Blenheim, receive invitations down the line. The message would come through that such-and-such a family would like to invite two sailors for the weekend, which was lovely because it was usually very pleasant, rather wealthy families, with large houses, who would really look after you.

"Most of the upper classes had French or Greek. I still had enough schoolboy French to get by, 'la plume de ma tante', and such. I couldn't really get on with French, but I didn't know any Greek. I'd learned ancient Greek at school, but that had no relation to Modern Greek, except the alphabet. I sat down to study it, and became quite proficient in the end, and then this job came up in the Greek Navy.

"I can't remember why the Lieutenant wanted rid of me. I was just a Leading Hand, and very junior, so there was no question of answering back to him or being rude to him or anything, you'd be put in jankers. Jankers was a punishment for those who'd committed a military offence. Anyway, he was determined to get rid of me, and I'd learned Greek. So I was off, transferred on loan to the Greek Navy. I had to join a Hunt-class destroyer in a dry dock in Alexandria.

"I remember it was a hot day, it was always hot in Alexandria, when I went to join the destroyer. When any ship in any Navy, well, any ship at all, is in port, there's a hand of some authority at the end of the gangway to stop unauthorised people just wandering on board, and he's called a quartermaster. In the Royal Navy, of course, he's always equipped with webbing belts and webbing gaiters, he's very smartly dressed. Of course, there was a quartermaster on this now-Greek destroyer, which had been called HHMS, His Hellenic Majesty's Ship, Crete. The quartermaster there was like some sort of beggar man, without proper uniform at all.

"Having turned up in pretty decent gear, we went up the gangway, turned aft to salute the quarterdeck which was the proper thing to do, I think the quartermaster wondered what we were doing. The Greek Navy had very different disciplines. And then somebody took me down below to the mess on British ratings. There were six of us – there was me, two coders, two bunting tossers – those who signal with flags, they're called bunting tossers, and another radar operator. That was really my home for the last couple of years of the War.

"Crete was a Hunt-class destroyer, originally HMS Hursley. My job was to maintain the various radar sets on board: one air-to-sea set, one gunnery set, and one IFF, that's Identification, Friend or Foe. Through IFF, you could send signals to any aircraft anywhere near you, in Morse code, and you'd get back an answer telling you who they were. That was all right, I could do that.

"I did, one day, fall foul. I failed to remedy a fault on IFF, but fortunately, it wasn't German aircraft. The Captain was called Theophilides, he was rather cross with me at the time. However, that only happened once.

"The whole time, the Greek destroyer that I was on was frequently working with one other of the six destroyers given to the Greeks by the Royal Navy. Almost always, all hands were dragged into going ashore. Towards the end of the War, we were busy in the Adriatic, running supplies and guns in to the partisans in, what is now, Croatia, Bosnia, Slovenia, they're all separate countries now. While we were there: picking up these stores and supplies in Alexandria, taking them across the Med, up the Adriatic, the Germans were still in occupation. When we slipped in to some little creek of the Adriatic, it was a case of all hands on deck to quickly, quickly get the stuff off the ship and to the partisans; whatever rank you were, you'd be pulled up to act as a porter. By now, I'd become a Petty Officer.

"Then, occasionally, we'd be running stuff in and we couldn't get back out for some reason, mainly we were choked by the German e-boats, which were very powerful, heavily armed, very fast. Some of them had torpedo tubes on, others just guns.

"I do remember the Germans had various purges where they'd take over one of the Greek islands, and commence to fortify it or to do something to it. Chios was one place: one of the larger islands the Germans had moved onto, and we tried to dislodge them, and we got a good hiding. Our ship was attacked by e-boats, we had a number of casualties. Fortunately, I was not one of them. Yes, that was Chios. But for the most part, we were just skating from island to island, raising the spirits, letting the islanders know that there was an armed resistance still fighting for their people.

"There were lots of things that were surprising to me, as a middle-class boy, brought up in England, not used to having brothels on every corner. What surprised me quite a bit was, in all the brothels in the islands... If you go into an English restaurant, sometimes on the walls they have lists of all the dishes you can have... On the islands, in the brothels, on the walls were pictures of the girls. Like a menu. I remember on one the islands round Turkey, you'd find several girls' pictures, and two or three small boys'. Which was a shock.

"I remember in Mytilene, practically in Turkey, at the end of an almost-fjord of Turkish water, was an old castle. The whole place was full of castles. They had several brothels in this old castle. It was a different time, and a totally different way of life.

"Sometimes, we'd be landing supplies for the partisans and have to stay for several days. When you had to move, you had to move quickly because the Germans were still very active.

"As the War petered out, there were a few English people with the partisans but they were properly organised. There were many things there was no record of at all. I must be one of the only Englishmen, I suppose there were a few dozen, who actually fought against the Russians. When the War finished, when it was coming to an end, the Russians were keen on – wait – I haven't told you about the Revolution, have I?

"There were, of course, communists in Greece; they'd become very strong. After the War, Stalin was very keen on gaining control of Greece, as he had gained control of Bulgaria and Romania. He sent a small column down from what we now call Kosovo into, if you can imagine the mainland of Greece, peppered with these small islands, across the top is like a ribbon of Greece, where Thessaloniki is, that's where they were going to gain access to Greece.

"I remember, Piraeus was the port of Athens, it was about eight miles from the city on the tram. We spent a lot of time in Piraeus. When the Greek Revolution was on, we used to get the mail from time to time. On every Greek destroyer, there was a similar complement of half a dozen ratings, Petty Officers and such. Stalin sent forth his forces from Bulgaria, to show the Russian love for the Greek people. I remember on one occasion having to take mail ashore, and the royalists, who were desperately trying to keep an alliance against the communists, were shooting up and down the street. And we were, at that time, known as British ratings, on a British ship, friendly to everybody. I was taking this bag of mail ashore, which we'd carted up from Alexandria, and they all pointed their guns up in the air and stopped shooting – until I got back to the ship and then they started again.

"I do remember, it was later... The Greek Communist Party managed to take over the military barracks in Piraeus. We had to stand off-shore and shell the barracks. That was when we stopped being everybody's favourite boy.

"Along the shore, one night, there came a boat. There was firing all along the front, and there were two or three small girls aboard, dressed in rags, they were prisoners from some atrocity that had been perpetrated. These girls brought these notices out to the ship: the communists had put a price on our heads. That was very unnerving. Anyway, we knew that that was it, they didn't love us anymore.

"There was a funny incident which happened around this time. We were going down the coast to a place which was named for a time when the Ancient Greeks and Persians were fighting, about two thousand years ago, a naval battle was named after this place – perhaps it was Salamis. What happened was one Greek Petty Officer, whose name was Metaxas, and one other rating somehow got left behind when we moved out, and we had to go back to get them. They were probably at some knocking shop, or something. Captain Theophilides handled the destroyer like a taxi. He would charge up the harbour, and put on the brakes at the last minute, trying to avoid collapsing the whole jetty.

"On this occasion, there was a long wooden jetty standing out from this place, and this little, fat Greek Petty Officer, with the attendant rating, was standing at the end of the wooden jetty, waiting to be picked up. The Captain turned the ship and reversed it in, so that the blunt end, as it were, came into contact with this long wooden jetty. We moved it up out of the water. The rating, on the jetty, was pushing against the ship, pushing against a thousand-tonne destroyer, under power. We'd never seen anything so funny in all our lives. Obviously, nobody was hurt, and Captain Theophilides regained control of the ship, the jetty bobbed back into its original position, and the men regained their feet.

"I was telling you about when we faced the Russians, when they came down. I had a Sten gun issued to me at the time. The Russians fired a few shots. We fired a few shots. It was just to let them know that there was some armed resistance there, not a welcome. It was a demonstration, really.

"At one point, somehow, I got a touch of malaria. I was in hospital in Malta. When the War finally finished, whether a whistle went or what happened, everybody ceased fire, the German stations had to surrender, of course. In Crete, there were several instances, due to, more often than not, one man, who just would not surrender and wouldn't let the others surrender. They went absolutely wild. Fell to their basest instincts. They would move into villages, shoot all the men, rape all the women. Something had to be done. The Second Front had started. The Germans had gone wild.

"And this led to the dreaming up of a scheme called the Independent Guard Company, which took under its wing anybody who was able to walk and carry a Tommy gun, or a Sten gun. And what a strange lot it was, RAF people of all regiments, all sorts of others. I think in the mob I was with, there were about fifty or sixty. I'd been discharged from hospital, and grabbed by somebody and put into the Independent Guard Company.

"We were landed in Crete, and were sent to go and clear up this one particular village called Kissamos. We had to advance on this village, and we had quite a battle. Our particular company of fifty-odd were under the command of a Lieutenant Cheeseman, I think he was Canadian. We moved into this village, I think Cheeseman was killed. He was certainly hit. That was quite a fire-fight. We suffered a number of casualties.

"We rounded up all these Germans, and the things they were doing were just monstrous. We took the civilian survivors back under guard to Souda Bay. There's a famous Suvla Bay in Turkey, to do with the Gallipoli campaign, but this Souda Bay had been our headquarters in Crete when we were there before the Germans arrived.

"The Independent Guard Company had a lot of British, and many other odds and sods; a very motley crew of chaps who were on our side. There was a heavy influence from the Greeks. The Greeks had suffered terribly from these appalling things the Germans had been doing, and there was no instinct to give any sort of understanding to the Germans who'd committed these acts, you see. So, the next day, the Germans were lined up behind the hospital and we shot the lot. I'm going back over seventy years. We took prisoners but we didn't keep them.

"And that was my twentieth birthday.

"So, the end of the War. It all seemed to be terribly disorganised. We'd won the War, we all knew that. Of course, we had huge numbers of Englishmen dotted about all over the place, they had to be got back to England.

"One thing does, looking back, surprise me. We didn't seem aware. Although we might be sitting around the mess table, we didn't seem aware that there'd be one place that was empty, because we'd lost somebody. It could have been any of us. It could have been me... but we were missing somebody, and we didn't seem aware, somehow."

Ted

"I WAS BORN IN AUGUST 1942. Many early nights were spent in the next-door Anderson Shelter, which we shared. In terms of early memories: after the War, when I was about five or six, I saw buses in Southampton with the windows still painted out from the blackout days.

"My education started at the village primary school. I went to prep school for three years. By this time, singing lessons had started. I took the entrance exam for Winchester College Chorister School. I failed first time but passed the next year. The choristers at Winchester College are called Quiristers rather than choristers.

"General education suffered a bit as we spent too much time learning and singing sacred music and oratorios.

"Probably the most memorable occasion in the three years I was there was with Isobel Baillie, soprano, and Alfred Deller, countertenor. Alfred Deller produced the most incredible sound we had ever heard from an adult male voice – falsetto. We were in Winchester Cathedral with the Hallé Orchestra, conducted by Sir John Barbirolli – which was such a memorable experience. We performed to a packed cathedral.

"So, age took its toll and my voice broke. Having passed the eleven-plus, I went on to Churcher's College in Petersfield for two and a half years. I did a bit of singing there, Gilbert and Sullivan school productions, etc.

"In terms of GCE and O-Levels – of course, we still had GCEs and O-Levels – I got enough to go into the sixth form. Unfortunately, halfway through the first term of the sixth form, the county council who'd been paying my grant – it was a fee-paying school – stopped the grant, so that was rather the end of my grammar school education.

"So, what to do next? Well, it looked like a service life. Both my parents had been in the Navy, but the Navy didn't appeal to me. So I applied for the Army Apprenticeship Scheme, which I joined in 1959. Discipline was no problem after two lots of boarding school. Plenty of the other boys found it a major struggle.

"I qualified as a tradesman in July 1961. I received a new uniform, as a Lance Corporal, with a good conduct badge on the left sleeve – which was a Lance Corporal stripe worn upside down – also known as a G-flog.

"Then, I spent three years, plus, in Dortmund, Germany with 256 Signal Squadron, attached to a 47th Guided Weapons Regiment Royal Artillery, which was equipped with Corporal missiles. It was pretty stagnant there in terms of career advancement.

"Eventually, I went back to Catterick for a Class Two course which, fortunately, I passed. I was posted then to 3Division HQ and Signals Regiment in Bulford, Dorset, still as a Lance Corporal.

"That leads us to the Commanding Officer's Interview, which all newly arrived NCOs had to undertake. I complained that I was not being employed in my trade, which I'd just qualified in as Class Two, and that I was stuck making cups of tea and lighting the fire. It didn't impress me a lot.

"Rapidly, I was marched out of the Colonel's office. As I got close to the Squadron Office, there was a bellow from the veranda, summoning me to come quickly, in rich military terms. And I was straight in front of the Squadron OC, a Major, who, in fact, I met much later in life, when he was the Mayor of Southend. I didn't reintroduce myself at that point. I didn't like him the first time round.

"At the time of my complaint, he was astonished that I would have the nerve to grumble to the Commanding Officer.

"So I said, *'Well, I mentioned it here, but nobody took any notice.'*

"He said, *'Well, we'll put a change to that. Go back to the Squadron Lines and the Troop Staff Sergeant will be waiting for you.'*

"He was, and within hours I had signed for a detachment of radio relay, which is what I had come to do – complete with a driver and an operator, who had the worst reputations in the Squadron. Nobody wanted them. I inherited them. So I thought to myself, *'we'll nip this in the bud straight away.'* As such, before we actually got started, I had a quiet word.

"*'Now listen,'* I said, *'you two have pretty bad reputations, for whatever reason, I don't know and I don't care why. I'm here because they think I'm a nuisance. We are going to show them we can be, and will be, the best detachment they've got.*

"*'So, you,'* I said to the driver, *'you get on and get that bonnet up, let's have the oil checked, the battery, all the fluids.'*

"I then turned to the operator, and said, *'You and I will get all the equipment off, check it, make sure it is as it should be, etc. etc.'* Which we did, and we all got along famously from then on.

"We were sent on numerous jaunts, because they thought we wouldn't like it. But, of course, we thoroughly enjoyed it. We had ten days at the World Gliding Championships in South Cerney. We set up communications and the public enclosure and otherwise, did very little for the time we were there.

"Much more challenging was something that happened in August of 1965: we went to Libya. King Idris was still on the throne. Libya was friendly. It was the last major exercise held by British forces in Libya before the overthrow, and the turmoil, which largely still exists. We worked at putting in a link between RAF El Adem and the British garrison in Tobruk. I was in El Adem.

"We worked a three-way shift. If you don't know what a three-way shift is: you work one afternoon, have the night off, work the next morning, have the afternoon off, and then work for the night. You then get a day and a half off. It works out quite nicely. I had plenty of time for swimming, trips here and there. The three of us decided – having acquired the use of a Land Rover – that we would go to a place called Bardiyah, up near the Egyptian border. Bardiyah had been a German submarine base during the Second World War. The land was very high, and below was – almost a concealed harbour, with a very narrow entrance, it was well protected by the cliffs.

"There was a little room up there, with a grille in its doorway, and a little boy on sentry outside. On payment of a few pennies, he let us in and showed us this place. It had been a prison for half a dozen or so British soldiers, during the War. There was an incredible mural painted on the wall in charcoal, water and, as we soon gathered, blood. It was extraordinary.

"By this time, I'd been elevated to Full Corporal. When we got back from Libya, I spotted an advert on the noticeboard looking for volunteers to go and become a Gurkha. So, in January, I was posted to 17 Gurkha Signal Regiment in Seremban, Malaysia. This was towards the end of the confrontation with Indonesia, in January of 1966.

"During the time there, I actually did very little because we only had two lots of equipment which generally, the Gurkhas looked after. I did a short-term posting – three months – to 246 Gurkha Signal Squadron in Shek Kong in the New Territories in Hong Kong. The idea was to try and establish a fixed radio relay link between Shek Kong and the military headquarters on Hong Kong Island. Because of the terrain, it was considered impossible.

"I should explain, radio relay is a fixed radio link, capable of carrying telephone conversations, teleprinter circuits, none of which you can hear actually going over the air – it's all sub-audio, concealed within the signal.

"To everybody's surprise, it worked, so there were pats on the back all round for us and for the men at the other end. We were very pleased. And with that task over, I went back to Seremban for Dashera, which is a major Gurkha festival. Dashera culminates in the head-chopping of countless chickens, geese, goats – the final bit being a full-grown water buffalo, whose head is taken off in one blow by a Gurkha using a very large kukri. In one swipe, off it comes. There's blood all over the place. Then, they hurriedly collect up some of the blood and pour it down the barrels of the weapons of the regiment for good luck, good shooting for the year.

"The night before, we'd been invited to a large assembly hut, with a stage, where the Gurkhas did lots of traditional Nepali singing and all the dancers, dressed as women, were Gurkha soldiers. They kept us well-lubricated. Every time you took a swig of your drink, someone came along and topped up your glass with a mixture of beer (usually Tiger beer) and Roxy, the Gurkha-issue rum: a lethal combination.

"We were not allowed to leave until we'd all been up on stage, and had a shot at this dancing. It must have been in the early hours of the morning. Well, I suppose we all made total fools of ourselves but the Gurkhas thought it was funny, so we just did it. And we were nursing hangovers the next day, just in time for the head-chop.

"In the January, I was posted to 248 Gurkha Signal Squadron in Singapore. I went to Nee Soon Camp, which was a place I actually stayed overnight when I was posted to Malaysia in the first place.

"From there, I returned to Catterick for a Class One course for six months. Having come back to Catterick, I had to change from Gurkha uniform back into a British uniform. But in the Gurkha uniform, I would have looked rather out-of-place with the rest of the squaddies.

"Anyway, I'd come back for this Class One course and I failed at the last post, as did two others. We were all very cross because we'd failed on a piece of equipment that we were all perfectly familiar with, and had worked on for most of our military careers. But – we had upset the instructor somehow. So, when we failed, we were duly retested and – we again failed. So we agreed, when we got back to our units, we would complain again. Which we did.

"I went back to Germany. Not only the same city, but also the same camp and barrack block, again with the Royal Artillery. This time, they had Thunderbird 2 missiles.

"Two, maybe three weeks later, I was back on the course at Catterick and – lo and behold – so was one of the others who had complained. We tacked on to the group that had been running behind us. We received some credit for completing the course earlier, finished up, and we both passed with Class A.

"The former instructor had been posted to the Outer Hebrides.

"Later on, under defence cuts, the whole unit was returned to Shoeburyness, near Southend-On-Sea. We combined with another signal troop and two Royal Artillery regiments, and were turned into different units. So, one regiment became the 36 Heavy Air Defence, while I joined 260 Signal Squadron. By this point, I was a Sergeant.

"When I was taken into the mess for the first time, it was a lunchtime and I was told I wouldn't be going back to work in the afternoon. What I didn't know was that I wouldn't be in a fit state to do so.

"A senior warrant officer told me that I was entering the most exclusive club in the world: the Sergeants' mess. It certainly is a very different atmosphere from anywhere else. And it's very handy because you get to meet all the other senior ranks, with all the different cap badges and so forth, and you can learn a lot from their experience. They could teach you things about dealing with men, for instance, which, up until then, you might not have needed to know.

"I was demobbed in July 1969 having decided that I was unlikely to gain any further promotion. Unfortunately, or fortunately as it may have been, they moved the goalposts, and Class One technicians were allowed to progress beyond Sergeant a year later. This was because there was such a backlog of Sergeants waiting for progression, and people were going out when they didn't want anybody to leave. Anyway, I'd already left by the time that decision was taken.

"I joined the Plessey Company, which was a major communications supplier for the Ministry of Defence in the UK, and in many other countries around the world. I shared digs with another guy who'd been in the workshop where I'd been in Shoeburyness. He'd gone to Plessey about six months before I got there.

"So, here we go, countries I worked in...

"Jordan, from the January. I worked there for six months on a job with another engineer. We were installing ground-to-air UHF radio for the Royal Jordanian Air Force at sites all over the country. The works were all underground and then covered in sand to 'disguise' them from the Israelis. It's very difficult to disguise anything when there's a very large radar scanner roaring around over the top of you. The work was primarily supervisory as we had a team of Jordanian technicians who actually did the hard work.

"Sometime in the late February or early March, there was a bit of a skirmish going on with the Palestinians. Very often, there was the sporadic sound of gunfire at night. We didn't take a lot of notice. We just got used to it. However, the customer advised us that we should probably leave the country for a week and we didn't need any further persuasion. Off we went to Beirut.

"There *are* worse places to escape to. We took advantage of the time off and decided to see a little bit of the country. We hired a car – it was a big American heap, with a foot-operated handbrake – which was impossible. The car was heavy and cumbersome, so we traded it in and got a Volkswagen Beetle, which was much more civilised. We tried to get up to the Cedars of Lebanon, but I'm afraid we were beaten back by the snow.

"We went to Baalbek which, I think, is largely destroyed now, but then had some magnificent remains left amongst the ruins of the old city. Truly, worth a visit. We also went to the Casino Du Liban – not to gamble, but to see a stage show the like of which I had never seen before, and am never likely to see again.

"It was about two and a half hours long, this show. There was a great walkway, which came right up through the stalls and back round to the stage. At one point, elephants came, walking around through the audience. There were motorcyclists, speeding along. In one of the acts, three white horses, galloped at full speed across the stage – well, this gives you some idea of the scale of the stage and the production.

"Later, a huge tank of water came up through the floor and there was an underwater ballet with semi-clad females, cavorting in the water: all perfectly decent and respectable, of course. Every now and again, throughout the show, they rushed to the corner of the tank to breathe through an air pipe. It was quite staggering and ridiculously cheap. So that was our Beirut excursion.

"Jordan: well, everything went fine until July. My colleague was still having breakfast and I was about to go to work. Just as I got outside the front of the hotel, I was shot at.

"I thought, *'That's a bit antisocial.'*

"So, I went back into the hotel but I told myself that it couldn't have been as close as it felt. As I said earlier, there was often gunfire in the night, to which we paid little attention. So, I went outside again. And I was shot at again, but this time, they hit a pillar not far from me. Bits of concrete scattered around me. I realised they were serious.

"Well, that was it. Nobody was allowed to leave the hotel from then on. Suddenly, the place was full of Palestinians with guns. We didn't know what was going on. Some foreign nationals, other Arabs, were allowed to leave the hotel, but any English, French, Americans, various others – no.

"We managed to phone our customer to explain that we wouldn't be coming in to work for a while, because we couldn't get out of the hotel. The customer went on to let the company know what was happening, because there were no mobile phones or other electronic items – none of that existed. Communication was by cable. But the only cable access was in the post office, which was some way away. So the bosses wouldn't have known what was happening to us.

"We were allowed to wander around in the hotel, use the bar, for a couple of days. Then, suddenly, we were all herded down into – what had been a nightclub – in the basement of the hotel. Round all the supporting pillars, which were holding the weight of the hotel above, were canvas satchels, which were packed with explosives. We then realised what our fate might be.

"There were plenty of international newsmen there and we got friendly with a few of them. The one I particularly remember was from the BBC. His name was Sandy Gall. I believe he wrote a book about it later on.

"By now, our passports had been taken away and we had to fill in Prisoner of War forms, including contact details for those who would need to know what had happened to us, back home. It all started to get very frightening.

"We were allowed to sleep in our rooms at night, and we were fed, but we weren't allowed to go as far as the restaurant. They brought a meal to us once a day, for which, the hotel charged us handsomely when we paid our final bill.

"On one particular morning, we heard a lot of banging on the doors and, *'Get up, get up, get up!'* There was a man with a big gun, looking very fierce, so we did as we were told. We were taken into a conference room, where the TV crews had got their cameras set up. Well, we didn't know what was going on. We were all stood in rows, and suddenly, there was Dr. George Habash, who was the leader of the Popular Front for the Liberation of Palestine.

"He talked to us – talked *to* us, not *at* us – for about twenty-five minutes and it was all perfectly sensible. He told us about the way the Palestinians, generally, had been treated by the rest of the world. And then, he apologised for our being held hostage.

"When he retired from the room, it was immediately filled with Iraqi soldiers, who were armed to the teeth. They had taken over responsibility for us. We were allowed back into the main body of the hotel.

"The British Embassy staff eventually appeared – because we'd received no word from them in the time we were locked up, of course – and they made all sorts of waffly excuses. They told us they had got our passports. So, we said we'd like to go home, rather than go back to work again. There was still a lot of fighting going on between the Palestinians and the Jordanian police and armed forces. In due course, we got our passports back. We booked flights to go home. We were taken out by Red Cross flights to Geneva and then, on an Argentinian airline, a 707 – the most exotic aircraft I'd ever seen. Anyway, all we cared about was that it got us to Heathrow.

"Two of the main airbases of Jordan are worth commenting on. One is Mafraq and the other one is H5. Mafraq had Hawker Hunter jets and all the pilots behaved like RAF Officers and dressed accordingly. At H5, the aircraft was a Lockheed Starfighter and they all behaved, spoke and dressed like Americans. Most peculiar.

"I stayed in the officers' mess at Mafraq, and I was classed as a pilot so I could have two fried eggs for breakfast. Otherwise you just got bread and coffee. We didn't stay at H5 because the Americans were working there and they wouldn't stay anywhere overnight, except in a hotel, and they had been in the same one that we were in. Every morning, we flew up with them in an ancient Dakota from the military airfield, which was also – at that time – the civil airport.

"On, to Algeria: I was informed, not long before I got there, that nobody spoke English in Algeria. All anybody spoke was French or Arabic. Well, I had schoolboy French from many years earlier, but that was about it. Anyway, off I went.

"I found out what the job was, but I'd never seen the equipment before in my life. I'd be installing HF radios for the Algerian Customs Department. HF radios are used when you need to send the signal all the way around the world. The system would go all the way around the borders of the country, including in and around the Sahara Desert. I went to places like Tamanrasset, which is now a watering hole on the Paris Dakar Rally. Tinduf, Colomb Béchar, Oran – which is on the coast, where the French had settled many years before, and a couple of other places. The job went on pretty well. It was very, very, *very* hot so we started work early. I hired local staff to do all the hunting and heaving, putting up aerials, etc. and the rest of the work was connecting up the coax cable. Once it was all in place, we could just plug it in.

"I woke up, it must have been the middle of the night, I suppose, and I was freezing cold but pouring sweat. Well, I couldn't get back to sleep. After a couple of nights of this, I knew I wasn't well, and I'd had enough. So I booked the flight and I went back to Algiers. I spoke to the customer and explained. I couldn't sleep because of this illness, whatever it was. When I came back home, I phoned the company and they were very understanding. I saw my GP, and he recognised my symptoms as something similar to malaria.

"Well, I'd seen malaria in Malaysia. I hadn't had it myself, but I'd seen it. Matter of weeks after this visit to the GP, I went back to Algeria. The idea being: to finish the job.

"Well, within a day of being there, the fever returned. I knew I couldn't stay, so I came back home again. Once more, saw my GP and he said, *'Ah! Since I saw you the last time round, I've been in touch with the School of Tropical Medicine in London and they've given me the answer: it's called Relapsing Fever. It's caused by a minute, little fly, about the size of a sandfly – it's like a tiny speck of cigarette ash, you wouldn't even notice it – and it's only endemic in a couple of countries in North Africa. Algeria being one of them. Now, the cure is this... don't go there.'"

<Me: Oh, gosh.>

"Yes, so, if it affects you, don't go there. So that was the end of me in Algeria.

"Kuwait: I went there to fit out twenty French-made AMX13 mini tanks with new radios. All the cabling inside was French, but they didn't want French radios. I suppose it was because they didn't speak French...

"I also connected up the harnesses. To explain: a radio harness is used to create an interface between the cable and the radio. It's how the system links up. If you asked someone what a 'harness' was, they'd probably imagine a knapsack or a baby carrier. But it's also part of the communications system.

"Kuwait was a very dry country. Fortunately, there was an outfit called the Kuwait Liaison Team, British Forces, who looked after the technical teams. And they had a very nice, very *wet*, Sergeants' mess. They were allowed to take visitors on a Thursday. So that was me for the two Thursdays I was there. As a visitor, I was not allowed to buy a drink. I couldn't give them any money. They'd get the drinks in because they could use it every day, of course, so they wouldn't let a visitor get the drinks in. So those Thursdays were fairly fluid afternoons. And evenings.

"Nigeria next: I took a few trips to Nigeria. The first time I went to cover the commissioning of some radio relay equipment, which had just been lying there in containers. There was grass growing through the stock. We had to push past the grass to get to the containers. There was a big external air conditioning unit, absolutely monstrous size, with a pipe about fifteen inches wide feeding the air in and back out again. The air conditioning unit really couldn't manage. Part of the equipment kept overheating and going out of sync.

"That was a bit of a problem, so I got hold of the company. We were still only working on cable. No mobile phones or anything like that. I suggested somebody who knew the equipment should come and bring some temperature sensors. Anyway, out he came and we managed to arrange a fan inside the power amplifier to produce extra air, thus cooling the equipment down and making it work. Great relief all round.

"Plessey wanted me to obtain a letter of release from the Nigerian Army Signals who, of course, owned all this kit. This would help Plessey get their money because they hadn't yet been paid for it. Well, Nigeria was probably one of the most corrupt countries that I had ever worked in. Everything was 'dash'. Whatever it might be – *'you dash me, you dash me'*.

"For instance, you go to a pub on a Saturday lunchtime, for a beer and something to eat, when you go to park your car, a crowd of little boys would come up and say, *'You dash me, sir, I'll watch your car.'* So, you'd give them half the money then, and half when you came back. Because if you paid them all in one go, when you came back – all your wheels would be gone – that was just the way of things.

"I came home briefly and then I was sent back to do some more work on the original equipment. While I was there the second time, they wanted me to commission and check a load of radios, which had come out of Land Rovers.

"The equipment I was to check had already been checked – by me – a year or so before. So, I checked it all again and, in the course of that, picked up contact with my friend, Ian, from the company, who was now the Plessey agent in Nigeria – and doing very nicely, thank you very much. So he and I had a few sherbets together, and that was Nigeria.

"Iraq: this was when Iraq was still friendly. Two of us went there to demonstrate some radio relay equipment. We set up in two places, which turned out to be famous, or infamous, later on – Fallujah and Abu Ghraib – and that was where we set up the two ends of our link for the Iraqi Air Force. Why they wanted fixed link communications we didn't know, but we didn't ask.

"It was a straightforward job. We switched the equipment on. It worked. The teleprinters and telephones were all fine, but they wanted to run it for a while to make sure it wasn't just going to go off after a day or two, so we had to stay. And the Iraqis were the nicest people you could hope to meet in all the world, polite, hospitable, all spoke perfect English – we only had minimal Arabic, but enough to be polite – and they were very nice people.

"We took the opportunity to see the Hanging Gardens of Babylon, one of the Seven Wonders of the World. How it was ever made one of the Seven Wonders, I cannot imagine. It was a heap of rubble. We got taken around by a little boy, who we paid a little, and in broken English and a bit of French and a few other languages as well, he explained to us where the gardens used to be. There had been balconies, tiers, but it had become this – wreckage. What it's like now, after two wars, I can't imagine.

"We joined the British Club, which was a terribly-terribly British institution. Got the tie on, and we went on a river cruise one night down the Euphrates. It's worth noting that the Euphrates and the Tigris meet in Baghdad. All the Club servers were there and they had a barbecue kit. And we enjoyed this leisurely boat trip. We went under a bridge and we suddenly got great, big stones thrown at us. Of course, I'd been dodging missiles for a while, but it still came as a surprise. Anyway, all in all, a successful evening was had.

"At one point, we had to go to the Internal Affairs Department. We had to get our visas extended because the Iraqi team, although perfectly happy with the equipment, wanted us around a little longer. Applying for the extended visa took a day. Because they wanted to know – the name of your grandmother's milkman and... you name it, they wanted to know it. They went through these great manuals, checking all your details. Well, it took a day, but we got our visas.

"The other interesting thing there was that we were allocated a tame spy. Well, we noticed him on the second day there. He was in a grey Morris 1000. We'd seen it on the first day we went off to work, because you couldn't *not* notice it. When we came home, we saw it again. We thought it was strange. Anyway, going out for work the next morning, there it was again! So we set a little test for him...

"We got in a taxi, told the driver to take us to a restaurant. When we got there we asked the driver to wait for us and we went inside. We stayed in there for a little while, had a beer, and then came out. We looked around – lo and behold – there was our spy parked about six cars back, waiting for us to reappear. Any time we wanted to see the agent or talk about anything a bit sensitive, we just lost him by changing cabs, or going into a shop through one door and coming out through another. He was no expert.

"One morning, the hotel staff asked us if we'd fix a tape recorder they'd got behind the reception desk. We wondered why they'd asked us in particular and they said they knew we were engineers. Well, there was nothing in our passports to say that we were. It turned out that the tape recorder was being used to monitor our conversations from the phones in our rooms. We found that out by... don't ask how we found out.

"UK: I had six weeks at the Rover factory in Solihull. We worked in the special delivery section of Rover. If you got your car ex-works, that's where you went to collect it. Two blokes would spend two and a half days polishing just one car. They fitted these enormous spotlights on the cars sometimes. Whatever you wanted, it could be done. And it was a very pleasant six weeks.

"I spent quite a bit of time working on television transposers which were designed to change from VHF television broadcast down to UHF for local consumption. It was happening all over the country and it meant working at night because we had to wait until the television programming had shut down. Most of it had finished by 11.30 at night anyway. And that's when we started work on these aerials.

"I spent a long time in Cammell Laird in Birkenhead, working on an ex-Royal Navy destroyer, HMS Diana. HMS Diana had been sold along with HMS Decoy, both Daring-class destroyers, to the Peruvian Navy. We had to strip the equipment from the warship, and take it back to Ilford, where Plessey had their headquarters. It was all re-valved, re-sprayed, the full retinue, and then reinstalled on the warship. There were four of us most of the time, sometimes five. A lot of the work we couldn't actually do because of dockyard demarcation.

"We had to be very careful in the dockyard. We could not go near bulkhead wiring because if we did we'd have the shop steward jumping up and down, and smacking our fingers because that was a dockyard electrician's job, of course. He would deliver the cable to us with the appropriate plug, and that was the extent of our contact with it all.

"I went out on the sea trials, which was quite exciting. To the measured mile, up on the Clyde, they fired the big guns – which made a lot of noise. The most interesting bit of the trial – frightened the life out of everybody – there was a weapon on the rear of the ship, which the Royal Navy called the Hedgehog. It was three big barrels and they fired something a bit like a dustbin, up over the ship's mast and it went off a bit like a depth charge for Anti-Submarine.

"To test the hull of a destroyer, they used this weapon and sailed over the explosion. And the sound when it exploded… Equipment started uncoupling. Light bulbs fell out of the ceiling. It was… it was quite funny. Importantly, the hull was intact.

"Anyway, I was there for five years. Just before I left there, I got married. Dorn and I had been together since, well, I was still in the Army, in 1969. I'd got a new job coming up and you could only have a lady with you if she was your wife.

"So, one Saturday morning, I said, *'Would you like to get married?'*

"*'Well,'* she said, *'why not?'*

"So we went down to the town hall that morning and we were married on the Thursday. We had about six people there, which suited us.

"The job was in the Far East, in Brunei. Brunei is an Islamic Sultanate, on North-West Borneo. It was moderately laid back. Alcohol was available in the shops.

"The job was looking after communications, initially in a workshop, for the Brunei Armed Forces – all three services were all Army, there was no separation of services in Brunei.

"I was never designed to do repairs. I didn't like the look of green boxes on a desk. I'd rather have been doing installation and commissioning, which is what I'd been doing all my life up until then. I was eventually able to persuade the chief engineer I'd be better doing those. So I was given the job of planning the installation of radios for the military police – the police station and their Land Rovers – the medical services, hospitals and their ambulances – the fire service and their fire stations and engines – and, of course, the base stations, which is what everything revolved around. It was a huge amount of work. So that kept me quiet for quite a long time.

"Masts, signal masts, were a bit of a headache because they came, about two hundred feet of kit, like a Meccano set. We'd fit them all together and then get a low-loader and a crane. Then, we would get to site, having had the civil work done. Sixty foot was the highest tower we had – and they had to put the aerials on top. In addition to the installation work, we had to fit out all the vehicles.

"Trying to fit an aerial on the fibreglass roof of a fire engine is a bit difficult – they want a metal roof – but we found a way of doing it. There's very little metal in these Bedford fire engines. They were all fibreglass and wood in the cabs.

"While I was there, Dorn was with me, and we had free accommodation, free electricity, free water, free telephone, no income tax, no national insurance: a wonderful life. And we managed to visit Australia, Malaysia, Singapore, Hong Kong, and the Philippines, at various times because we were there for twenty-one years altogether.

"Socially, we were... well-integrated, I think that's the right way of saying it. We were members of the Yacht Club almost as soon as we arrived. It was *the* social place for ex-patriots. Later, we joined the Non-Descripts Club – which was for almost anybody. We were in the Teachers' Club. We belonged to the Dramatic Society, the Music Society.

"I also joined the Ex-Services Association of Brunei. This was a largely ex-pat organisation, similar to the Royal British Legion. I became Poppy Appeal Organiser in 1976, and was later President, for around eighteen years. The Poppy Appeal is the only charity which is allowed to solicit funds from the public in Brunei, by kind permission of HM The Sultan. No doubt, this is in recognition of the assistance that British and Commonwealth troops had rendered to Brunei during the Second World War and in later, smaller conflicts.

"Then, I had a heart attack. We'd only been there about four or five months. I was off the road for a while, had to stop smoking cigarettes from probably fifty a day, lose three and a half stone, and start doing regular exercise.

"I started hashing. Hashing is a lunatic activity that involves running. It happens all over the world. The nearest one to here is somewhere down the A38. When I was in the Far East, they started the Interhash. Every two years, there's a gathering of Hashers from all over the world.

"Well, I was fortunate enough, I went to five: Kuala Lumpur, which was the first one, Hong Kong, Jakarta, Sydney and Pattaya. Pattaya is a beach in Thailand. Now, these are as you may imagine, very fluid affairs, but you go running on two of the three days of the bean-feast. Whatever you pay to take part covers all your drink, all your food (apart from breakfast at your hotel) and it's enormous fun. You meet people from all over the world, all creeds, there's no bar on belonging. It's absolutely brilliant.

"My wife was very involved with the Amateur Dramatics. She used to do costume making. She produced a couple of Noël Coward plays in the local television theatre, and I was able to do the lighting in conjunction with the Brunei TV technicians with their big, monster control board. I just told them which light I wanted and where and they did it all. That was very good.

"We were still in Brunei but came home briefly for the VJ Celebrations in London. At that point, I was a member of the then British Commonwealth Ex-Services League Committee, now the Royal Commonwealth Ex-Services League. I was invited to be a guest of Her Majesty aboard HMS Britannia, to see the fireworks on the Thames. That was rather splendid.

"That afternoon, we were outside Buckingham Palace. There was a big stand and Dorn was with me, and there was a fly-past over the Mall, which is the way of things, at such occasions.

"I'd spent a most interesting evening. When the fireworks were about to start, the Queen and the rest of the Royal Family went up onto the bridge. I was, at that moment, talking to the Duchess of Kent. Her husband, the Duke, advised her that they were all going upstairs to watch the display, and she informed him that she was having a nice talk and was going to stay below. Which I thought was really kind. She's a beautiful woman, an absolute charmer. She was drinking orange juice while I had gin and tonic. I barely had half a sip when someone came up and refilled the glass for me.

"The following morning, Dorn and I were invited to a reception at the Queen Elizabeth II Centre, where the Queen would be wandering around, talking to various 'worthies,' which we were considered to be. We didn't actually get to meet the Queen, but I briefly had a nod on board Britannia the night before.

"Back to Brunei: Well, I suppose one of the highlights was on January 1st 1991, we were able to tell family and others that I had been awarded the MBE in the New Year's Honours. I knew in the October, but you're on virtual pain of death to tell anybody apart from your wife. So, we had a few close friends around for a drink with the kids, Alec, who we had adopted, was with us and we had champagne and orange juice – bit of a bash on New Year's morning. I was tickled pink. My wife even more so, I think. I was the first ex-patriot ever to get an honour in Brunei.

"I got on very well with the High Commissioner because of ex-service things that I'd been involved in, and I helped him out a few times here and there, rescuing people and getting them back to their countries to save them from difficulties, and I suspect he recommended me. But you never see your own citation. The only thing you get is similar to the article in the newspaper, which is about four words. Mine was 'For services to the British Community in Brunei.'

"With that, I suddenly became President of the local ex-pat football club, Grand Master of the Hash – that was something else they decided I ought to be. And my hashtag – you see, there's a scurrilous newsletter every week from the Hash, there's never foul language, but it... gets pretty close. And everybody's got nicknames, which are known as hashtags. Well, mine became Lord Ted.

"Around this time, prohibition came. Brunei was getting more and more Islamic. We were given three months to get our social club closed and get rid of the stock. So we made full use of those three months. We got loads of extra stock in while we could, and then bought it from the club to take it home. Anyway, it soon transpired that the Chinese had set up a distribution network. They brought the beer into the country, all wrapped up in black bin liners, and delivered it to people like me. So they were the wholesalers and a few, like me, became retailers. It was two and a half times the price we'd paid before but there was no shortage of customers. I used to deal with fifty or sixty cases a week.

"Any customers who came to me were told exactly when to arrive. Not a minute before, not a minute after, because I didn't want any two customers bumping into each other. As soon as they got into my carport and turned their lights off – it was like clockwork: boot up, beer in, money over, exact money please, boot shut and gone. Then, the next customers would be there within four to five minutes. Never got caught, fortunately, otherwise life would have been a bit different.

"And then, there was a big surprise. After almost twenty-one years, I was made redundant. It came as a shock, but I think my wife was getting a bit fed up with the changes that were coming. Life, generally, was getting more oppressive, so she really wanted to come home. Dorn was older than me, and she wanted to come home and be here with her children.

"We had a round of farewell parties. Extremely fluid. One thing was strange: under the new rules, as a foreigner, you could come into the country once or twice a day, with twelve cans of beer and a litre of spirits. So a lot of people would go out on a Saturday morning, go to Malaysia – which you could get to in a water taxi in about twenty minutes – go to the shop there, twelve cans and a bottle of gin, and then come back. You'd have to fill in a yellow form, but all that was allowed. It was strange but it kept the supplies up for these parties.

"About three days before we left, we went to our final Annual General Meeting at the Yacht Club – I'd spent a long time on the committee and had been involved with the Yacht Club for years – and, out of the blue, Dorn and I were made Honorary Life Members. We were numbers eight and nine in the history of the Yacht Club, so that was quite an honour. I've still got my membership card so, if I go to Singapore, I can use about three clubs over there. I can use another two in London, on the strength on my Yacht Club membership.

"So, we returned to the UK. We went to Hampshire to live with my sister for about three months. Of course, I had no home, no job and was in my fifties. Well, two families in one house is all right but it's not ideal. Dorn wanted to come to Devon. She had her daughter in Torquay and our son, Alec, was in Exmouth. I thought I'd be just as well out of work in Devon as in Hampshire. I'd been turned down for any kind of benefits. I was told I wasn't entitled to them, having been out of the country for twenty years.

"Anyway, during the time I was out of work, I used to go to the pub in the village every day from five until six to see if there was any work going. I met a guy in there who did telemetry for what was then the National Rivers Association. It's all part of the Department for the Environment, Food and Rural Affairs, now.

"He told me that telemetry was the metering of water flow, etc. and that all the information was sent back, via radio, to a central control point. They got all their staff from an agency, he told me. So, I thought I might have a go at that. Got my CV typed up and applied to South West Water.

"On the Saturday morning, I'd been in town and I'd visited the RBL Club in Exeter. I'd first joined the Legion in 1961. In the Exeter Club – which is not there anymore, now it's a nightclub – I met Keith. We got talking. He asked me where I was living and when I told him, he said, *'Oh, we need a Poppy Appeal Organiser there.'* I asked him what the post involved. *'Oh, not a lot,'* he replied."

<Laughter from me>

"So he invited me to the Legion Clubhouse here. He told me how to find it because I wouldn't have known this place existed, and when I came on that Sunday lunchtime, I transferred my membership from Exeter, and became Poppy Appeal Organiser for my village.

"At the time, I only needed around twenty-five Poppy tins for my area, so it wasn't overly strenuous. That number grew to sixty-odd, spread over a very large geographical area on the eastern side of Exeter.

"Back to South West Water: I was interviewed and started working for them. The wages were... Well, we could live. Just about. We decided that paying rent was getting us nowhere. Unbeknownst to me, Dorn had found a mobile home not far away. I came home from work one day and she suggested we go and take a look at it the next morning. For the two of us, it was perfect. I went to the bank and made the arrangements and that was it. We moved to – what is still my home today.

"In South West Water, I worked largely on radio surveys. Checking that the fixed radio link could work – from the reservoir, pump station, sewage works, water treatment works, anywhere with SWW plant – making sure the data could be sent back to the control room in Exeter. Of course, there were over a thousand sites belonging to South West Water, so that kept me very busy.

"I went on to actually overseeing the installation of all these sites with radios, radio aerials where applicable, and the telemetry, with a local company who I'd vetted. They were only a three-person company but very reliable and knew what they were doing. That was for Devon. Cornwall, we had a slightly bigger company, who'd done work for SWW in the past and there was no reason to change them.

"Meanwhile, I'd gone up to County Vice Chairman in the Legion. In fact, I would have gone to the Chair had I not been so busy with South West Water. I had been asked to form my own company, doing all this commissioning work, and I was quite happy. It meant, however, that I had to turn down the chance for advancement to County Chairman because I just did not have any free time during the week. And the County Chairman, unfortunately, does have to go off and do things. Still, I felt very privileged to be asked. So, I came out of that loop but I became County Recruiting Officer for six years. I was in the County Executive Committee and I enjoyed that.

"I was Contingent Commander of a review in Paignton by the Royal British Legion which had the Duke of Kent in attendance. We were taken in hand by three Royal Marines for ten minutes before the Duke arrived, so at least we didn't look too disastrous when we did our march-past.

"And then, in 2005, I took early retirement.

"Back to the Legion: through Keith, I'd been put forward as a candidate for Deputy Vice Chairman of Devon County. I was already on the County Committee and a representative of the Otter Group. Anyway, I was put forward and, to my huge surprise, I was elected as Deputy Vice Chairman.

"Also, as Poppy Appeal Organiser, my area was growing like topsy. My tins were scattered around Exeter, but if I hadn't had Dorn, I couldn't possibly have stayed on top of it all. She did all the record keeping. As we drove round – I planned the route – but she'd tell me the can number, and the appropriate number of poppies for businesses and door-to-door collections.

"Unfortunately, Dorn died in 2011. I did get a very nice letter from the Chairman of the Poppy Appeal Committee but I couldn't do the work without her.

"In this Branch, of course, I've remained on the Committee. I was Chairman for five years. I'm the Vice President of the Branch. And I do still have a small Poppy commitment – fourteen tins, which I take charge of.

"And I think that's it."

Fred

―――――

"I STARTED OFF LIFE as a cadet at school – the Combined Cadet Force. In those days we had an Army, a Navy and an Air Force Cadet Force. And I was in all three of them.

"Well, you had to do a year in the Army cadets and then you were qualified to march and things like that, and if you wanted to change, then you could. So, I changed to the RAF, for a year, but I didn't like that. So, I ended up as a Navy cadet.

"I worked in industry, for a while, as a trainee chemist. Then, when National Service came along, of course, I went into that. I was eighteen and in the RAF. And I rose to the dizzying ranks of Senior Aircraftsman, based mainly in Northern Ireland. I was with Coastal Command as a medical orderly. In the last year, in fact, the squadron was doing weather reports and we went out to Australia for six months.

"It took us eight days to get to Australia. We got out there on Shackletons. A Shackleton is a four-engined aircraft, like a Lancaster bomber, with counter-rotating propellers. When we flew out to Australia, we stopped off in Idris in North Africa, to refuel. And from there, we went to Baghdad, would you believe? This was in the fifties. We had an Air Force base there with a fantastic swimming pool, I remember that especially. From there, we went to Karachi, I think, and then to Changi Airport in Singapore. From there, we went down to Darwin.

"During our time in Australia, we flew down to Melbourne with the squadron. I had relations in Melbourne, but apart from that, nothing happened, really. Of course, in those days, and we're talking about '54 here, Darwin was just like a cowboy town. There were boardwalks, just one main street, and stuff like that. A couple of years after we were there, a big cyclone hit Darwin and now it's a big city.

"Anyway, on the way back, we did the same thing. We stopped in Singapore, and in Colombo – that's in Ceylon, as was, and then Sharjah, in the desert, before heading back to Northern Ireland.

"It was when I was doing my National Service that I first saw a dead body. Even in those days, the IRA was active, and the service police used to carry live ammunition. They had Sten guns.

"I was on duty one day and we got the call. This SP – they're military policemen, service policemen – he was sitting in a guard room, bored out of his brain – he cocked the Sten gun, it wasn't loaded, but he put a magazine on it. Now, with these things, what happens is: when you pull the trigger, a bullet is loaded from the magazine and it fires. So he was bored, just mucking about with his mate, and he shot him through the chest.

"So, I came upon this scene. I'd have been almost nineteen then, and I'd never seen a dead man before. It wasn't a massive wound. It was just a hole in his chest. But he was the same as me, he was just a nineteen-year-old National Serviceman. I think the guy who shot him did a year for manslaughter.

"Shortly after that, a Neptune, which was an air-sea rescue aircraft, went into the Irish Sea. There were seven of them on board. They took the bodies to a sort of mortuary, which was in a Nissen hut, and the MO said to me, *'I want you to go out and measure these lads up for the undertaker.'*

"So, I was there. It was night time. I was on my own. I mean, I got through it but it was a shock. Tragic, all seven of them died. I don't know what had happened, whether they were flying too low, or what, but they crashed. Terrible.

"In Belfast, on the airfield... You can imagine how big an airfield is, can't you? Like, somewhere like Heathrow, if you can picture that. Anyway, the railway line ran along the bottom of the airfield. The line went from Belfast to Derry. When I was coming back from my home in Liverpool, I used to get the boat to Belfast, and the train to Derry, and get off at Ballykelly Airfield.

"So then, I'd have to get a message to the medical centre to get the ambulance driver to come and collect me. Exciting times.

"Do you know, I've never been to Southern Ireland? I've been close. I keep saying, *'one of these days,'* but, not yet. I had a mate who worked in the medical centre, Joe, he was from Wexford. Nice chap. But, no. Never been to Southern Ireland.

"Actually, that's not strictly true. On Saturday nights, we used to go to a place called Muff, which was just on the edge of Derry, just on the border of Northern and Southern Ireland.

"But I enjoyed Northern Ireland. We had two years of National Service but really, it was like a holiday. Pay was bloody awful. Other than that, I enjoyed it. Just – not enough to sign on.

"When I was in Northern Ireland, in the medical centre, we had a Sergeant. He was my boss. Fast-forward ten years, I was a medical student, and I applied for cadetship in the RAF. I had to go to Brize Norton for an interview, and who should be in the medical centre? Sergeant Whatever-His-Name-Was. Small world, isn't it?

"Anyway, I went back to industry as a trainee chemist, did that for a few years and I didn't really like it. I thought, *'bugger this'* and I gave it up. I had five O-levels. You had to have five, in order to go on to Birkenhead College, which is where I went to get my three A-levels, which I got in a year. From there, I went to Liverpool Dental School."

<Me: Really? So you became a dentist separately from your time in the Army?>

"Yes. Well, in actual fact, I applied for the cadetship because I was married by this time, with a family, and you could get paid as a Lieutenant, or equivalent rank, if you had this cadetship. Anyway, they didn't want married men at the time, so I tried the Navy first. Then, I tried the Air Force, where I encountered Sergeant Whatever-His-Name-Was. And then I thought, *'Bloody hell, I'll join the Army, then.'* Which is what I did, for five years.

"After four years of being stationed in Germany, I thought, *'This is better than working,'* and I wound up with a permanent commission.

"We came back to London, I was with the Gunners in Woolwich. No, I wasn't. I went to Aldershot. And then, I went to Hong Kong for three years. While I was in Hong Kong, I learnt to fly. I got my private pilot's license. And crashed an aeroplane.

"We were doing some circuits and landings, and we tried to land on one circuit and a wheel fell off. It was hanging under the wing – well, between the wing and the tail. So, we did a three-sixty – this was at Kai Tak Airport. So, we did a three-sixty, came back and fortunately, we were going in the right direction. You see, when we landed, the aeroplane bounced on the runway and shot off to the left, and we ended up in a big mound of earth. If we'd gone the other way, we'd have gone into the sea.

"I did a spell in Brunei with the Gurkhas. When we were in Hong Kong, we used to cover their dental treatment. It wasn't really a choice: it was either Brunei, attached to the Sultan's Army, or it was Nepal, at the military hospital out there. So, I went to Brunei. In those days, the Sultan of Brunei had his own army, but the dental officer, who was in his uniformed army, was a chap I knew from university. While we were there, I went water-skiing with him.

"After Hong Kong, I went to Woolwich. That was... well, I nearly left, actually. There was an advert in the Journal from a chap looking for a partner in the Isle of Man. I wrote to him, said I was interested, and he replied that he was coming to London the next week, so we could meet up then. Just before he came, he wrote again and said he was sorry but he'd given the job to a colleague of his. So, in the event, I didn't leave.

"In the seventies, I was based at the hospital in Musgrave Park, in Belfast. There were two dental officers serving in the Army who were brothers, Brian and Lenny. Lenny was a semi-professional fly-fisherman, and Brian lived just down the road from where I was based.

"There was a woman who used to come to the Legion here, and she had lived at Limavady. She was in the Air Force, I think. Well, anyway, when I was a National Serviceman, in the fifties, I was based in Limavady... well, close. I was based in Ballykelly – which is a couple of miles outside Limavady.

"In the mid-seventies, I was based in Woolwich, but I had to go over to Northern Ireland to attend some clinics. I was over there for a couple of months. In that period, the Air Force base at Ballykelly had closed and been taken over by the Army. I knew a dental officer over that way, and so we arranged to have a catch-up. We got a car from the motor-pool.

"The reason I'm telling you this story is: the distance from Limavady to Ballykelly is only about two miles, and there'd been a gap of twenty years since I'd last been there, and – it was exactly the same. It hadn't changed one little bit. I couldn't believe it. It was like going back in time.

"I was in Woolwich then until 1976 and I was doing ordinary dentistry, which I was getting fed up with, so I thought I'd go over to the surgical side. I then embarked on a six-year career of surgical training.

"I remember once, I was playing golf in Guildford. It was an Army match, and I was playing for the Dental Corps. And George Smith was there and asked me how I felt about going to Berlin. I said, in between shots, *'I'd better have a word with my wife, Audrey, about this.'*

"When I went into work the next day, there was a letter saying, *'You're being posted to Berlin.'*"

<Lots of laughter>

"So, I went to Berlin, to the British Military Hospital there. And that was where I treated Rudolph Hess. He was in Spandau Prison and whenever he was ill, he used to have to come to the British Military Hospital. He came in one day with some problems with his teeth, and I treated him.

"This was all before the Berlin Wall came down, of course. I was with 3 Queens Regiment as the dental officer. I went on a four-week course to learn German. And while I was down there, I met this Canadian helicopter pilot.

"One weekend, he said to me, *'I'm going to go up in this helicopter, do you want to come with me?'*

"We went up in this little helicopter called a Hiller. It was like a big glass dome, really, with the blades on the top. I said to him, *'What happens if the engine cuts out?'*

"*'Oh,'* he said, *'that'll kill you.'* After a lengthy pause he said, *'What you've got to do, if the engine stops, is you've got to change the angle, the rotation, of the blades. And you've got about five seconds to do it. Then,'* he said, *'what happens is the blades just keep rotating and you'll glide down to earth. Here,'* he said, *'I'll show you what I mean,'* and he cut the engine off.

"We dropped like a stone! And then, all of a sudden, we just slowed down and glided to the ground. That was an experience.

"And then, I came back. Finished my training at Charing Cross Hospital, got my fellowship, and I went back to Woolwich.

"I did a year there, but I'd lost the will for a khaki uniform, so I thought, *'bugger this'* and I applied for a job as the oral surgeon in the Solomon Islands, in the South Pacific. Once there, I spent three years in Honiara, Guadalcanal.

"When I first got to the Solomon Islands, everything was new and exciting, sometimes amusing, but after three years, it got to be a real bore – because, you know, you'd organise a meeting with the Ministry of Health, on a Wednesday, and they'd turn up on Saturday. Because it was just island life: if the weather wasn't right or... Time didn't really exist over there. So it was very frustrating to try and get anything done.

"Theoretically, my job there was to train a new oral surgeon, and he arrived about a week before I left.

"I did a tour of the Gilbert Islands. The Gilbert Islands were British protectorates then. When they declared independence, the Gilbert Islands became Kiribati. But I was there, for a while, to set up the medical centre. That was interesting because I went out with a medical team to a place called Marakei, which is a little island out in the middle of nowhere. There weren't any roads or anything like that, so we used to get around on motorbikes.

"When we stayed on Marakei, we used to sleep on a thing called a kia kia, which is a little thatched hut with no walls, like a platform, and the toilet was out over the sea.

"On the way out, we went to an island called Nauru, which came into existence from a mound of bird droppings. So it was like a huge pile of fertiliser, which they sold off and made a lot of money out of it. It was very much a throwaway society. If the washing machine packed up, it would just get thrown away. It was that kind of disposable society. And everyone was fat. Which was strange because of the way they used to get the coconuts.

"They used to put plaited palm fronds around one ankle, then put the frond around the base of the coconut tree, and tie this plaited thing to their other ankle. They'd have a similar arrangement for their hands, and then shinny up the tree to get the coconuts.

"I, and the rest of the medical team, went to what was called the Weather Coast. Guadalcanal is quite a big island but there's only one road along the northern edge of it. It ran from the airport, all the way along, until it petered out in the jungle. But then, it was all forest and everything all the way down to the southern coast, which was the Weather Coast. We went by boat to do some dental extractions down there in the bush. I'd never been so seasick in all my life. It was an interesting experience but I wouldn't want to repeat it.

"Guadalcanal, of course, was where the Japanese were, and they used to fly from Henderson Airfield to Fiji, Australia, Singapore. We used to go on holiday to a little island, I've forgotten what it's called but it was about twenty minutes away by light aircraft. And it was the archetypal paradise island. It was fantastic. There was a hotel there – I mean, none of these places was run very well, they were a bit, sort of, hit and miss – but this one was great. I did quite a lot of scuba diving. I played a bit of golf. There was a golf course in the Solomons just down the road from where I lived, but the greens were actually sands. Like a flat area of sand that used to be raked regularly. It was quite difficult to play on but you got used to it.

"When I was at university I had a mate called Dick. He did ten years in the Navy and, to cut a long story short, he ended up as a lecturer at Hong Kong University. Anyway, while we were in the Solomon Islands, he came to visit us. I always remember, one day, he had to go to the bank, and on the island there was only one bank. It was the Australia and New Zealand, A&Z, bank. So, I took him down there and as we were standing at the counter, Dick said to me, *'Can you believe it?'* – there was a bloke standing next to him who used to share digs with us when we were students. How strange is that?

"This guy, Peter, was a doctor. He'd trained in medicine in Liverpool and gone on to work for the World Health Organisation. Now, the Solomon Islands were rife with malaria, and Peter used to run the malaria programme, and he was in Honiara on a visit.

"Then, after three years, my contract was coming to an end, and I nearly went for New Zealand next. I have a brother in New Zealand. But I thought I'd have a look through the Journal, and they were advertising for an oral surgeon at the hospital in Hanover. It was a civilian post. I knew the guy who was in charge, a chap called Clive, and I wrote to him and said I was interested in the job. And he wrote back. He said, *'Unfortunately, we've just given it to Tony Quant.'* That's Mary Quant's brother, by the way. Anyway, he went on, *'Would you be interested in coming back into uniform?'*

"By this time, I was fifty-three and officially, too old. It wasn't too much of a problem, he said. So, I rejoined the Army.

"I was immediately posted back to Woolwich. Did another year there, and then, the Gulf War started, in 1990. I went to the Gulf War with the field hospital for six months. It was quite interesting. Unremark-able, from a surgical point of view. There were a few road traffic accidents but no real war wounds while I was there. We had one Scud missile aimed at us, but it missed, fortunately.

"We were billeted in a camp. The Saudis employed a lot of foreign workers and they had this camp made up of huts, with showers and everything. It wasn't fantastic but it was all right. Just before the War started, they decided that because we didn't have any air-raid shelters, they would supply us with these damn-great big sewer pipes. We had one, and we had to sandbag the ends, because otherwise, they were just open to the outside. In the event, it didn't happen so we never actually needed them.

"But we used to have to wear our NBC suits (Nuclear, Biological, Chemical Suit) because there was a danger of Saddam sending over nuclear or biological warfare, but that never happened either.

"Of course, the Gulf was dry. We had this drink called Near-Beer, which was basically alcohol-free beer. It was awful stuff. I think it had a diuretic in it.

"I remember one day, when we were in Iraq, it was a Saturday morning and there was a knock on the door, and this half-Colonel (Lieutenant Colonel) came in. He was a *frightfully* nice chap. He was a bit of a – what would you call it?"

<Me: Rupert?>

"Rupert. Well, he'd been hit in the face playing polo. He'd fractured his zygoma (cheekbone) and they'd put a plate in. This would have been just before the War started.

"Later, I was a member of a golf club, and he was the chairman – this chap with the plate. But even more of a coincidence is when I got to

Berlin, he was there as well. And, would you believe, he'd been hit in the face again, playing polo? He came to see me in Berlin, because the Germans wanted to take the plate out, but it wasn't really necessary, so we didn't.

"Anyway, Dick, my mate from university, had a son called Ian. Ian had been to Cambridge and was an officer in the REME. He was on a short-service commission. When Ian was at Sandhurst, we went to his passing out parade. And who should be in charge at Sandhurst? This chap with the plate. I'm trying to think of his name...

"As soon as I got back to England, I was posted on to Germany, to Rinteln. I did three years in Germany and they made me a consultant. And, funnily enough, my neighbour was Tony Quant. By this time, Hanover had closed down.

"The Air Force wrote and said they wanted an oral surgeon, a consultant, in Wegberg – in the RAF Hospital there. And so I went to Wegberg for three years 'til 1995. After that, I didn't have anything to do, so I came back to Catterick. Wegberg closed down in 1996, and I should have retired around the same time but the Army asked me to stay on for another year.

"In Wegberg, whenever we had any in-patients to treat, we used to send them to the American hospital in Wannsee, and I used to go over by plane to treat them. I'd go up on a Monday. Have a clinic on Tuesday. Stay with them on a Wednesday and then come back on Thursday. That would be a normal week in Germany with the Americans.

"That was interesting because they used to do everything differently from us. But it was good, I enjoyed it.

"All in all, I spent about fifteen years, off and on, in Germany. Rinteln, Hannover, Wegberg, Berlin. When I first went out there, Germany was smooth and sophisticated, clean – this was in the late sixties. The women were very well-dressed, the shops were lovely. What was interesting was, by the time I left, it had really gone downhill, like England.

"It was a pity, that. You could see the change. You could go away for three or four years, come back and you could see the change in the culture and everything.

"And then, I came here. The best thing about having been around the world a few times is – I've no desire to go on holiday. It's too much hassle."

Sid

"I HAD VERY LITTLE EDUCATION before I went to the grammar school.

"I was the first boy – the first common boy, with his backside hanging out of his trousers – to go to the grammar school. My parents were poor. My father was a labourer, and my mother looked after my sister and I with whatever money we could come by; there wasn't a great deal in those days. So, for a ruffian like me to be put into grammar school was unheard of. It came about because of the 1944 Education Act, which opened up the grammar schools to the ordinary people – and I was the first one in. I was eleven years old, good at maths, useless at languages, and rather nonconformist, which resulted in many detentions and canings.

"You can imagine the headmaster:

"*'Boy, I don't want you. We don't have boys like you... You're going to learn Latin.'*

"I didn't know what Latin was.

"*'You've got to learn French.'*

"I didn't know any French.

"*'And English language.'*

"There were two-hundred boys – well, two-hundred-and-one boys, one of whom didn't know what a verb was, didn't understand Latin, and wasn't really wanted in the school in any case.

"It would be exactly the same if you were to go to a village in some far-flung country, on your own, and they were all talking, you would not understand what they were talking about, would you? That was my education. I didn't have a clue: verbs? Adjectives, nouns, pronouns? Not a clue.

"The teacher would say: *'Come on, then, where's your homework?'*

"And I'd reply that I was sorry but I didn't know how to do it.

"I was sent straight off to the headmaster to be caned. He would tell me between strokes that I must learn more quickly.

"I did make some good friends while I was there, but I was always outside the headmaster's office. So, I enjoyed my social life, but not my education.

"I got expelled quite a few times. Well, in those days, we didn't have holidays. Couldn't afford them. Couldn't have even one day off, but my mother wrote to my headmaster and said, *'Sidney will not be in school on Friday. He's going to Ramsgate,'* which was about thirty miles away.

"And so the headmaster called me through and said, *'Boy, you cannot have Friday off.'*

"So, I went home to my mother, and she said, *'You will go because I've paid for the coach.'*

"So, what do I do? Do I obey my mother, or the headmaster? Of course, mother comes first. So I didn't go in, but when the next school day arrived, he called me through. *'Expelled!'* he said.

"And from then on, it was decided that something must be done. My father and his four brothers were in the Navy during the War, so it was obvious: I had to go into the Navy. I was no good educationally or technically, and I couldn't go in as an Officer, but I knew I wanted to do something with my hands. I could do that as an Artificer, also known as a 'Tiffy'.

"The headmaster told me, *'You will never, ever pass the exam, boy.'*

"Well, I took the exam and passed. Everyone was astounded. My headmaster was delighted because he'd got rid of me, but by then, of course, he'd had to take on other common boys.

"It was then that I found out I needed to be 100 pounds in weight and 5'2" tall. I was fifteen years old, 5'1", and weighed 99lbs."

<Me: At that age, I'm pretty sure I was heavier. And shorter.>

"Well, with good, nourishing service food, I grew a bit and never looked back.

"I joined HMS Fisgard, in Torpoint, Cornwall, for the first sixteen months of my five year Royal Navy apprenticeship. I received my first wage packet. We were paid six shillings a fortnight (equivalent to thirty new pence), which was to be used on necessities and luxuries.

"I was a rebel but when you're in the services, you have not got a chance to push back. Everybody's waiting for you. In case you're not marching properly or if you're not marching fast enough or in the right direction, if your boots are dirty, or you haven't had a shave, they'd notice and if they wanted to, they would have you.

"And many times I had it. *'Double-time round the parade ground, with the rifle.'* The discipline is meant to break you, meant to make you fall in line.

"It took me some time to get used to the way of things, but a couple of sentences with the cane soon taught me to conform. Service personnel under the age of eighteen could be caned in those days. In the Services, canings were vastly different from the mild form rendered at school. Each stroke was intended to draw blood.

"I was taught to use my hands. It was a harsh training. You spend four months with your tools, cutting through metal, filing it smooth, you use callipers and you learn forging – joining metals together.

"You know the classic Spanish swords? They're renowned for being superior swords. They are created by beating metals together. They spend ages, just with heat and a hammer, and we were taught to do it. So you thump it and bang it around and you can make metal bigger and bigger and bigger. If you've got a big job to do and you need a large piece of metal, you'd join pieces together.

"One of our poor chaps, and I remember this always, was hammering away at the metal and – bang – he took his toe off.

"On another occasion, there was a chap using a shaper, a machine that cuts metal off as it goes to and fro. Somehow the machine broke, and the shaper went through him – half a tonne of machinery – *through* him. You'd hear about these things and you'd develop a sense of where you were, where you needed to be, what you were doing next. It's very important to be aware of your surroundings when there's machinery, metal and moving parts involved.

"We had to make some of our own tools, like chisels and spanners. Of course, the compulsory marching, parading and discipline honed our minds. The aim of our role was to undertake Naval maintenance, keeping it all working and, when it was broken, to mend it the best way we could.

"Trips out of camp were few, because we couldn't really afford much from our pay. Toothpaste, soap and washing powder, along with buying replacement clothing, took most of our wages. But I do remember splashing out one weekend.

"We walked in to Torpoint, caught the ferry across to Devonport, had a meal in a café, popped around the corner to a little pub which would serve us (underage) with two pints of beer. We smoked our three Woodbine cigarettes and then came back, on the ferry, to camp. We'd wait another fortnight for our next pay packet and, then, perhaps we could afford a few luxuries.

"On another occasion off camp, we were stopped by the local Bobby for not having lights. We were returning to camp in the dark, having been to Whitsand Bay on borrowed bicycles. Fortunately, he took pity on us and let us on our way without reporting us.

"I was once, unexpectedly, ordered to get ready for a coach trip and was taken to Dartmouth College, home of the Naval Officer training. I was to be interviewed. The interviews didn't continue once they found out that my father was a common labourer.

"I had a few days' leave between each of the four four-monthly terms and after sixteen months, having decided my specialisation, joined HMS Caledonia in Rosyth as an Ordnance Artificer Apprentice. For the next two years and eight months, my role was to specialise in theoretical, technical and practical ordnance, gunnery control and ASDICs (Sonar)– looking after gunnery and torpedo equipment, and all the associated things that go BANG.

"I couldn't swim when I joined the Navy, but my two chums, Loll and Bill could. The camp had a beautiful swimming pool and I was soon encouraged to learn to swim. I took to swimming underwater for long periods of time, diving off the 5m board and becoming a member of the water polo team.

"I've never been shy of volunteering especially when Shallow Water Divers were needed. I was up for this especially because it would pay me an extra penny a day if I passed, which I did. You remember, I was only getting six shillings a fortnight, but with an extra penny, I could buy five Woodbines and two or three matches.

"The first part, and most difficult and claustrophobic for most, was putting on the full waterproof suit and the big metal helmet with its airline hose. In addition to that, the visor was blacked out and we were thrown into the water to undo knots in chains. In this darkened state, orientation was a problem. It was almost impossible to know which way was up or down, or to know how deep we were. Fortunately, I was able to manage despite the disorientation, and welcomed my pay rise.

"Another time we walked the few miles to Kincardine, had a few beers, excitedly turned out every gas lamp we came across, plunging the High Street into darkness, and happily walked back to camp.

"Teddy Boys were attacking individual Tiffies ashore in Dunfermline, the local town. One weekend, six hundred of the eight hundred Tiffies on camp went ashore and sorted out the problem. The two hundred remaining only did so because of their on-camp duties, being on watch, sick or excused. Every available Tiffy did his duty and supported his mates. This comradeship and support continued throughout service life and into retirement. I still correspond, after almost seventy years, with a fellow Tiffy called Bob.

"Now, on board ship, it's not like a cruise liner. Everything's tight in there, and you've got to get in these little, awkward places and I'm – I used to be – six foot tall. The bulkheads in Navy ships were set about 5'9", so that's why I always stoop. I was always banging my head. I grew from 5'1" to six foot very quickly. Good naval food, you see.

"I loved my Navy life because it taught me comradeship, fellowship, dealing with people. I had great chums. And that's how it was. No matter what happened, you were with your chums.

"I remember one time when I was looking after two big turrets. I had a leading hand who, with a couple of – matelots, shall we say – gunnery ratings, went ashore one night. He came back on board, went to bed, got up in the morning. And they were going to charge him with being drunk on board, but they only approached him five or six hours later, the next morning. They didn't charge him when he actually came back on board.

"They called me as a witness. Of course, there I am – I've got the turrets that need maintenance and cleaning, and I'm in charge of these guys. I dictate what we've got to do. So, in effect, this leading hand works for me. Of course, I looked after him. Because, I thought, if I let him down, he'd let me down later on, and after a good sleep, he was working well.

"I don't know if the person who wanted to get him charged was trying to get at him, or me, but he was fantastic, a great worker, he could do anything I asked. And because he and I built up that rapport that you could only get in the services, we understood each other.

"You hear of it on the news, in places like Afghanistan where they will do anything for their mates – it's how it is with service people. And it happens in civilian life, I know it does, but in the services... it's unique.

"The fifth year of the Apprenticeship was the year of the examinations. It was the year when all theoretical learning was tested. I was granted my preference to join Chatham Division, one of three, with Portsmouth and Devonport, the other two. Chatham was a good choice for me as I was born and lived just ten miles away. I went ashore and home from there at every opportunity.

"This fifth year was to be spent at sea, so I joined HMS Jamaica, a Colony Class Cruiser. We were forever at sea undertaking sea trials and visiting many European coastal places: Tromsø, Trondheim, Oslo, Sundsvall, Helsinki, Copenhagen, Scapa Flow, Antwerp and finally, through the Kiel Canal in Germany. We were the first RN naval ship to pass through there since the end of the Second World War.

"I remember being on board ship... One of my mates was in a turret – a turret has big guns at the top, and through the ship is a big tube to the turrets and the guns. Well, the tube is in an outer tube. So, in between, one part is moving while the other isn't. So, this mate of mine was in the gap between the tube and the outer tube, and for some unknown reason, the turret started moving. And there he was, jammed and he actually got rolled, round and round and round while the turret was moving.

"He survived, but it gives you an idea of how vital it is to think about where you are, what you can do, and where your escape route is. Because I often had to go in, undo a hatch, get in there and deal with the equipment – our job was largely maintenance of the equipment. When it's rough at sea – a naval ship doesn't go in harbour when it's rough, it goes out – because you don't want to get bashed against the sea wall or into other ships. The rougher it is, the further out you go. But there's still maintenance to do, there's still work to do, and there are situations that are very dangerous.

"I must tell you about one incident. I became a Chief, going ashore, and I was working with torpedoes. These torpedoes were twenty-odd feet long, twenty-one inch diameter, tonne of TNT on the front, and I had to fuse it and put the gyros in. They weren't IT ones, they were run with a gyro – a gyroscope – that kept it on track. There was a lot of servicing of the equipment. In those days, all the moving parts inside a torpedo had dashpots. These little dashpots were like – you have them on doors sometimes, and greenhouse vents, where the door closes slowly – it's a little piston and cylinder arrangement, with fluid.

"Because of the metal composition of the torpedo, and the way it moves through seawater, and to allow for temperature compensation, you had to mix the water in the dashpot with methylated spirit. It worked out as one-part meths for three-parts water. As I was on maintenance, my job was to open up the dashpot, check to see the fluids were topped up, and top them up as required. We regularly looked at these. You could not assume that it would be all right. You had to be certain.

"So I got some meths from the stores, which I had to sign for, and I went to check the fluids. After the first one, I moved on to the next dashpot, opened it up, looked back, and there was a space. *Where's the bloody meths gone?* You couldn't be sure because there were hundreds of people on board ship but it seemed certain... Somebody drank it. Methylated spirit has quite a flavour to it."

<Laughter>

"But I loved the torpedoes. I only worked on them for about four months but the guys on the torpedoes had such a rapport, such a friendship and camaraderie from working together, we were great chums.

"It was someone's birthday and so a group of us decided to go ashore. This was a couple of leading hands and torpedo technicians, the normal run of sailors from the ship.

"We had a lovely time with the beer. Young chaps abroad. We were walking down a hill, laughing and joking, and one of these guys decided to jump on my back, to get a lift. And he just – jumped. Of course, we were walking down a hill so, as he hit my back, I lurched forward, he went over the top and – crash – he landed in a pile on the road. We'd had a few beers, so he wasn't hurt and we told him to get up.

"From all this, I got a reputation. The story went that he attacked me from behind and I *threw him* over my head, and slammed him onto the road. No one would try anything with me, because, of course, I could have them. I used that reputation a great deal. By then I was a big guy, six foot tall, twenty-five years old, and with this reputation – you don't use your strength because you don't need to. But, if you're in trouble, you can tell people to clear off.

"There was another occasion – we'd gone to Gibraltar on a ship. Now, there were a lot of ships. There were about four hundred Navy ships in those days. At least four hundred. When I joined up, I remember there was the battleship, HMS Vanguard, about eleven cruisers, two or three different classes of frigates and minelayers, minesweepers, hell of a lot of ships. You'd have difficulty counting twenty these days.

"What we used to do in those days – you had the North Atlantic fleet which was composed of the battleship, couple of destroyers, couple of cruisers, aircraft carriers, this was all at sea – not laid up in harbour. We would swap over with the Mediterranean fleet, so we would cover the Mediterranean and they would cover the North Atlantic. So, you've got two fleets, crossing over, as we always did, at Gibraltar.

"Now, sailors on one ship did not like sailors on another ship, so if you were in the pub together and there were two of them and three of us, they would have to go because it was *our* pub. If two more of theirs came in, there'd be a punch-up. Gibraltar was renowned for a good punch-up, particularly when two different ships got in there. More so when they had two different fleets in there, because then, they've got thirty ships, you've got thirty ships: you've got sixty ships! And tens of thousands of sailors in Gibraltar, all wanting beer and all wanting a fight.

"Now, who sorts the fights out? The Shore Patrol. And who is the Shore Patrol?

"The word came through. *'Chief – you're Chief of the shore patrol tonight.'*

"Oh, thank you. Because they'd pick on a ship, and they'd say they wanted a Chief and three ratings for Shore Patrol to patrol the streets and keep the sailors quiet. Of course, I didn't want to be on Shore Patrol because I knew what was coming. There were sixty ships *and* the Canadians were coming through. Awful.

"So I was there, Chief, couple of mates (you'd want them to be big), stick, boots, hat, white gaiters – walking down the street. I got to this bar, and there were some chaps from our ship, causing havoc, throwing chairs and all sorts.

"As Chief, I told the other two lads to get them out. Now, they didn't want the job either because they knew they were liable to get thumped – a bit like a policeman's role. And like a policeman's role, if there are three of you among four- or five-hundred, you haven't got much of a chance unless you take command of the situation.

"So, I stood outside the bar, and waited for the other two to bring them out. Inside was one of our well-known sailors, an absolutely lovely chap, who could *not* handle his beer. He always had to fight. So these two chaps go in and they start bringing the men out – of course, they don't want to come out – and I'm standing a little to one side, so they can get by me.

"All of a sudden, this guy, who was a very good worker on board ship, but was causing chaos because of the beer he couldn't handle – he sees me near the door – and because he'd dare not start anything with me (because of my reputation), he rushed past me and ran straight into a parked car. Fell to the ground, unconscious. So the two chaps carried him off to the compound. He recovered. During the night, he was taken back on board, charged with being drunk and disorderly – and lost his pay for fourteen days.

"But the guys looked at me in the following days. They were a bit dubious, a bit careful about talking to me. And what this chap had said was: *'I was in a fight in this bar, and I could see Sid outside. He sent two chaps in, who couldn't get hold of me because I was quicker than them, but when I ran out – Sid hit me.'*

"Now, he was a boxer, this chap, a bruiser. But instead of saying anything about the parked car, he said: *'Sid hit me bloody hard. Wallop. Don't you try anything with Sid.'*

"So, I was getting quite a reputation on board. And I lived with it. I knew how to keep out of trouble, but I was, inadvertently, making a name for myself. *I could hurl a man over my shoulder and into the road, I could knock a man out by standing at a door...*

"I was in Gibraltar when I bought my first very good camera, a 120 Rolleiflex film camera. I volunteered to be the ship's photographer. There wasn't any extra pay, but I did get some good perks.

"When we were in Naples, Lord Louis Mountbatten, the First Sea Lord, came aboard. I didn't have to stand to attention. No, not me. I just followed him around the ship, taking snaps and that was it. So, I had a good day off, while everybody else was standing to attention and being inspected.

"But of course, there was a lot of work afterwards because I had to develop all the film, sort out the prints, and there wasn't really a dark room on board ship. Because there couldn't be. It was a naval ship. So, I had to find some little compartment somewhere down in the bowels of the ship, where I could turn all the lights out and lock the door. In those days, I had to develop the film, make the prints and then send them off to the Admiralty. It was a good experience.

"I got to use my camera in every place I went to, and I even photographed a sailor's wedding. The sailor asked me if I'd do it, and I was happy to. It was nice to photograph such a happy occasion. That was in Malta.

"Back then, we never liked going to Sicily. Never enjoyed it because it was in the summertime and the locals thought it very, very funny to squirt ink out of their fountain pens (this is before biros, when pens actually had to be filled with ink) at us, from their second floor balconies. They found it very funny. All this ink made rather a mess of our white tropical uniforms and we had a job getting it out, and especially if we had to go on parade, it was terrible.

"We went to Izmir in Turkey. Izmir is the modern name for Smyrna, which was a Roman fort in Turkey. I went to Ephesus, which is a Roman ruin – the Temple of Diana, one of the Seven Wonders of the World, is there. And nearby, I saw my first camel train. A real camel train, going across the countryside! I had thought that camel trains only existed in Arabia but no, I was in Turkey when I first saw one.

"But Ephesus really interested me. I had an excellent camera and I took some wonderful shots. The main road was approximately a mile long and an earthquake destroyed Ephesus a couple of thousand years ago and it bent this main road in half. You could stand at the midpoint, look along the road and at the pavement, and every part of it was dead straight. Roman architecture – just incredible, it really fascinated me. That's where I got my love of archaeology, which I took up again in Hertfordshire when I retired.

"Like in Malta, for example, near Sliema, there are square holes cut in the rock of the foreshore, and people would sit in there for the waves to come over – for sea-bathing. And that was all designed and cut into the rock by the Romans. But there were people bathing and using them when I was there.

"After a while, I was flown back to the UK, to HMS Vernon in Portsmouth and the Royal Navy Torpedo Training Establishment. I was a Petty Officer, and I was told they had a ship for me to go to. I was well-pleased and asked them which ship it was.

" '*It's HMS Jamaica,*' I was told.

"Again! So, for the second time, I was going to HMS Jamaica, but it was good because I knew the ship well. Now, I – volunteered (I always volunteer, as you well know) to take the photographs on board. When we went into the Baltic Sea, there were lots of Russian ships around, this was during the Cold War, and it was my job to photograph every Russian warship and cargo ship we saw. It was a 120 camera, which I was familiar with, but it had a lens on it that was about a metre long. Now, the best vantage point for the camera to get a good view of port and starboard, fore and aft, is – at the top of the mast. There was a special place for my camera up there. We're now talking about one hundred foot off the sea, thirty-five metres or so.

"The Baltic Sea is rough at times and we were going off to Helsinki. Of course, there were Russian ships around. I had a special boatswain's whistle, with a signal that would come over the Tannoy. That signal was just for me. So, if I heard it, I would have to drop everything, pick up my camera, go to the Captain's area, put on my belt with clips, and climb to the top of the mast. Before the ascent, I had to make sure that the rotating radars had been switched off, because I had to climb over those, with the camera over my back, and a potentially rough Baltic Sea knocking at the sides of the ship.

"I had to use the clips to climb the mast. So it was clip-climb, clip-climb, clip-climb to the top. When I got to the top, there'd be a ship to photograph, perhaps a Russian Destroyer. I took some good photographs. But when our ship rolled, it was quite frightening because, suddenly, the water wasn't too far away. But I'd take the photographs and then, head back down to the bridge. On the way down, I'd let them know they could switch the radars back on again.

"I took it as read that the radars would stay switched off while I was at the top of the mast. But you can imagine, once you're up there, and there's an enormous radar, it just takes one idiot to switch it back on. Of course, they need the radar so they can see what's going on but not when there's someone on top of the mast. But it never worried me. I was never concerned about heights or danger and, in fact, that was all quite enjoyable.

"After the Baltic, we had to call in to Invergordon. This was in May 1957. Our ship was to join others in the fleet review, assembled to welcome home the Queen from a state visit to Denmark. It was the second time I was involved with the fleet review.

"My first was at Spithead in 1953, to mark the Coronation. We stood to attention for what seemed like hours. There were thousands of sailors, all on ships, all stood in rows, for inspection by the Queen. HMS Vanguard was there, our battleship. There were seven aircraft carriers, twelve cruisers, thirty-three destroyers, and hundreds of other smaller Royal Naval ships.

"Next stop, off to the Mediterranean again. I had three visits to the Mediterranean. This one was fun. We went to Haifa in Israel. We were invited to play on the first golf course in Israel, which was very enjoyable.

"We called in to Algiers. My chum and I met up with a couple from the French Foreign Legion and they took us to the Casbah of Algiers. It was quite something to see it in reality.

"We called in at Monte Carlo, where we were invited to see the Casino in the daytime. There were no croupiers but we did have a go on the fruit machines. The Monte Carlo Casino was *the* top place for gambling in those days.

"Another time, we went off to Cyprus. During that time there was trouble with the EOKA (Ethniki Organosis Kyprion Agoniston) rebels. The Turks and the Greeks had come into conflict close to Famagusta Beach. Today, Famagusta is pretty empty. There's lots of accommodation that is completely unoccupied.

"We went across to Famagusta Beach from the ship. We had knowledge of the EOKA terrorists, so we sent a couple of guards and put one at either end of the beach, with rifles, while we swam. The beach sand was so hot we couldn't stand on it. Beautiful in the summertime but so hot... you'd have to run across the sand to get in the water, and then run out of the water to sit down and have a couple of beers, all while the guards watched over us. And when we got back on board ship, we discovered that the guards didn't have any ammunition. They'd been watching over us with their rifles, and we'd been brought back safely, but they didn't actually have any ammunition.

"My next trip on the HMS Jamaica was to Alexandria, the port from which the Nile meets the Mediterranean. You could smell it thirty miles before you got there. The water was all cloudy and brown. So we knew we were going in the right direction. We were in there on a particular date: 26th July 1956.

"We were invited to go and play cricket. Of course, '*I volunteer.*' So, we played a game of cricket with the locals and, after the game, we could not get back to the ship. There were a million Arabs out there in the streets because Nasser was making his speech about taking over the Suez Canal. And we were in a coach in the middle of it. There was a lot of shouting. Really, I'm lucky to be alive because, had they known who we were, we might have faced a rather different outcome.

"We eventually got back to the ship, and we immediately sailed. After all his wrangling, Nasser had taken over the Canal and they'd started to sink ships. So, we sailed out. Now, that was in July and we stopped at sea until 6th November.

"On 6th November, the Royal Navy and French convoys came in at Port Said to give covering fire for the Royal Marine Commandos. I think it was all over in a matter of hours. Unfortunately, our gunnery was told not to fire the six-inch guns because we'd cause too much damage. It was a bit disappointing because, you can imagine, we'd spent all this time preparing for the invasion, you get there, only one hundred yards from harbour, everything is prepared and then – *'No. You'll cause too much havoc'*. So, the other ships took over and it was all done with quickly. There were a few casualties but it was sorted out very quickly.

"That was 6th November. By the time we got back to Malta, it was Christmas morning. We'd been at sea for almost six months. My wife at the time saw it on the news that our ship had sailed back into Valletta Harbour.

"After all this, we returned to Chatham and were decommissioned from the ship. We'd been away for eighteen months, and after a period of time at sea, the ship would get a new crew. As artificers, or Tiffies, we had our workshop in Chatham, which we went to every day, awaiting our next assignment.

"By then, I was a Chief, in the Chiefs' Mess. We were youngsters compared to many of the others. And of course, with new ships coming into harbour, the locals challenging the sailors, there was a lot of competition in those days, and the word went out: volunteers were needed. And I raised my hand.

"*'What are we playing today?'* I asked.

" '*Water polo.*'

" '*Yes,*' I said. '*Put me down.*'

"Hockey, rugby, cricket, football – I didn't like football a great deal, it didn't come up very often – rifle shooting, water polo... any sport at all, I would play. There were two or three others who always volunteered. In the mornings, we went to the workshops and – did very little – waiting for our assignment. But in the afternoons, we played sport.

"When we played sport, we got a free pint of beer the next day. What a wonderful payment system! We got quite good at all kinds of sports. And we enjoyed the beer.

"So, we were waiting for our next assignment.

"*Volunteer needed: We want somebody to be an armourer on Sheerness rifle range.*

"The elderly civilian armourer was doing the job but, perhaps, losing his finesse. He was about sixty years old, so they wanted a youngster who could learn and do exactly what was needed. Obviously, with the rifles, the pistols, the machine guns, whatever guns they had, you needed to be precise in taking care of the trigger and the sights. Using the rifle range, you had the Royal Navy Bisley Training Corps. Well, you've heard of Bisley, with the rifle shooting competitions...

"They wanted someone who could look after all the guns, to make sure they were exactly as they wanted them. The feel of the trigger has to be absolutely correct every time, and the guy who's using it has to feel comfortable – that he knows his trigger. Because you don't *pull* a trigger, you *squeeze* a trigger – it's very important that it feels right. And I was good at taking care of the guns, evidently, because they asked me back for a second year.

"Now, I didn't mind any of this because I lived nearby, I didn't have to go into barracks. I could drive my car over to the rifle range. It was only for six weeks in the summer, but what a wonderful six weeks it was. The guys would fire their pistols, Smith & Wesson, at targets, set at thirty yards; that was quite normal.

"The day started at about eleven o'clock in the morning and went on to about twelve. The local pub was an attraction, so we'd go there. The trouble was – they wanted me to do some work in the afternoon, so I couldn't drink more than two pints. The lunchtime drinks would finish around two o'clock but, you see, you can't fire a pistol for more than an hour, really, and so we were finished by three.

"When it came to competitions, with rifles set at a thousand yards, they really wanted good equipment. It had to be well maintained, and I took some pride in being able to look after it all properly and getting the triggers just right.

"Now, I'd finished with sailing at sea. In 1962, I was off to HMS Excellent (a stone frigate, shore establishment), at Whale Island near Portsmouth. The instructors there were renowned because it was the area where everybody doubles around. Even officers under training – on the double. I, as an instructor, was allowed to march. Of course, there were the top instructors, who made sure that the instructors marched properly. It was a very tight regime there. The instructors were known to be the Royal Navy experts in drill, in ceremony, and in gunnery. And from 1962, I was there, for my last couple of years.

"I was a technical instructor. I was in married quarters, living nearby. And I marched around. Every ceremony, really *every* ceremony, is trained for and rehearsed. Even the death of the sovereign is practised, every month."

<Me: Wow.>

"All of it. Including Coronation, death, everything – is rehearsed, so that if it happens – everything is there, ready.

"You see these spectacles on television, where they look smart and efficient and everything goes according to plan – it's really because it is, and always has been, rehearsed. Because you couldn't have something like that go wrong.

"Anyway, I was at HMS Excellent as a technical instructor. I was training mechanicians to do my job in three years. It took me five years. Still, you can understand, these were bright lads.

"You can imagine – you're always under scrutiny as an instructor because discipline and ceremony were very important. It had to be done right. There was no other way.

"I was nearing my time and thinking that my twelve years – Man's time – was nearly up. I looked at the noticeboard one day... and my name was top. I was the Chief to take the monthly parade. Of everybody, I was in charge. So, it was my job to report to the Camp Captain. Now, for a technical Chief, that job filled me with dread.

"I'm great with a rifle. I can do anything with a gun. A turret, no problem. A hundred-weight shell, I can do the lot. But I'd got to do a parade.

"Now, Tiffies are renowned for nonconformity. If you asked a crowd of Tiffies to march down the road, at the end of it all, some would be missing, others would be in the wrong step, some would be slouching, some wouldn't be marching to order, some would be talking, there might be people shouting at them – they would take no notice. Because our job was looking after the equipment on board ship. We didn't march. You can't march in a little compartment you've had to climb into, covered in oil and grease. You can't march from there. And they'd put my name at the top!

"One chap said to me, *Just make them do what you want them to do.*'

"So, there were a thousand guys lined up around the parade ground. I had the Chief GI, the top instructor, stood next to me. The Captain hadn't appeared yet. He had half an hour yet before he needed to be there, but the Chief GI was watching me. If I'd failed, he would have jumped on me, just as he would have jumped on anyone.

"So, they were all looking at me, all around the parade ground, and at the top of my voice, I called, *'Fall in!'*

"I thought about the advice I'd been given and I called them all to attention. I told them that they fell in in a very slovenly way. With that, I was going to clear the parade and call them back, to fall in again and do it properly. And so, I did.

"And they all fell back in again and it worked. It was wonderful. Quite soon, the Captain appeared. I saluted him, made my reports – however many were sick or excused – *'Parade assembled for your inspection, sir.'*

"The Chief GI, who was stood next to me, never actually said a word. I felt that I had control. They knew I had control. And as a Tiffy, I felt I shone.

"After that, I only had a short time left to complete my twelve years – Man's time. I was approaching thirty. Then I heard that they were going to stop the free rum ration and my mind was made up. That was the end of my service life.

"So, on my thirtieth birthday, I had no job and no accommodation. But within the month, I'd found a job and somewhere to live. I went into research and development and moved to a large company and there, in research and development, I found there were a hundred guys who were – you'll never believe it – most of them were ex-Tiffies. So, I was back with the people I'd been with all my service life, and it was great.

"Fortunately, in all my life, I've never been claustrophobic. When I left the Navy, I joined the archaeological society and they'd found a load of flint next to the river, and it was a flint-lined Roman well. Beautifully done, and you know what Roman work was like, it was beautiful.

"This well was quite deep. It was larger at the top and got smaller the lower down you went, barely a foot across at the bottom. So, I started pumping the water out, there was quite a lot of it to get through, but it was important so that somebody could go down there. We put the bucket down on a length of rope and, we didn't find a great deal of archaeological interest – a bit of a Roman pot and bones and some rubbish.

"On the last day, we'd cleared down to fourteen feet deep and I'd spent three weekends on this hand-pump, sucking the water away, so they asked if I'd like to go down to the bottom of this well.

"So, I thought... of course I would. I pulled out the bit of wood that goes across the entrance to the well and started down. Nobody else really wanted to do it, because can you imagine? You're going down into a hole, which starts out broad enough, but starts tightening up as soon as you're in it. There was a ladder and the bucket and a suction pipe – and once you're down fourteen feet, it's quite tight. When you look up, there's just a small circle of light above you.

"The claustrophobia didn't bother me because in my Navy days, I always had to go into small spaces. Just take the hatch-cover off and once you're in there, and you've got the equipment and the machinery going all the time, you get on with it. That's just how it was.

"I've always been interested in potholing. I've never really done potholing, as such. Always had too many other things to do, but I think I could take to it. Small spaces don't worry me.

"Heights don't worry me. In fact, when I moved to Devon, I stood on the top rung of a twenty-four foot ladder, holding onto the side of the house, and it was fine. I thought nothing about it. I wouldn't do it today.

"I fell off my roof once. The ladder slipped and I fell in front of the front door. It was only a bungalow, but I finished up on the ground – my leg was inside the metal ladder, between the rungs. I got up. Not a scratch. You hear of some people who have broken a leg or what have you. But no. Touch wood, I've been very fortunate and when I look back, I've thoroughly enjoyed lots of my life. Some things have been difficult, but for the most part, I've been very fortunate."

Mike

"I WAS A WAR BABY, BORN in Nottingham to Arthur and Doris, who were both teachers. At the time of my birth, my father, Arthur, had enlisted as a volunteer in 1939. Initially, he was a private soldier in the Bedfordshire Regiment. He deployed to France with the British Expeditionary Force and came back through Dunkirk, although, he never gave us the details. He was very intelligent and highly gifted. My father was subsequently commissioned as a Second Lieutenant, Royal Artillery, and was deployed to North Africa in an anti-tank regiment.

"I was on the way when he left for North Africa. He was taken prisoner at the Fall of Tobruk. He was shipped over to Italy and was initially in a prisoner-of-war camp in Chieti, which is on the bottom right-hand corner of the Italian peninsula. After the Italians capitulated, he walked out of the camp but was quickly picked up by the Germans. He was re-incarcerated and eventually put on a train, one of the cattle truck variety and was sent to Austria and then to Czechoslovakia. He finished up at his final abode as a prisoner of war, at Oflag 7E, just outside Brunswick, carefully sited between an airfield and an aircraft production factory.

"So they were bombed by the Royal Air Force and the Americans. Then, in May '45, he was liberated. He came home and I met him for the first time, when I was aged three and a quarter.

"Back on the home front, my mother got a job as a teacher in Suffolk when I was about eighteen months old. It was a small village, one room, one class, school in Little Saxham. I went to school at the age of two years and three months, purely as a child-minding expedient.

"The War still had a little way to go. I can't really remember it but my mother told me that I delighted in playing in crashed aircraft. There was a lake close to the village where the kids used to sail or paddle on a boat made from aircraft drop tanks.

"So, Dad came back and we all settled down as a family for a short time near Godstone in Surrey, and then we moved to Devon. My father was appointed the Deputy Superintendent of the approved school in Whipton. I became a Whipton Mixed Infant. After a few years, my father got a promotion and moved to another juvenile delinquent training establishment in Worksop, Nottinghamshire.

"Having re-established in Nottinghamshire, the county of my birth and home to my maternal grandparents and a handful of aunts, I found I was very happy in the north of England. Having gone through primary school in Worksop, I won a scholarship at the eleven-plus stage to Ripon Grammar School, in Yorkshire. On arriving there, I also became a chorister at the cathedral. I had a happy but unremarkable time at school as a boarder.

"I left after A-levels with the firm intention of becoming a veterinary surgeon. I applied to veterinary school and was offered a place but they suggested I take a year out between school and university to work on a farm and get some experience in animal husbandry.

"I decided to work away from home and got a job on a hill farm in Montgomeryshire. There were all the challenges of a new language and independence, but things were going to plan when, on a visit to my parents (by this time, living in Sussex), I met a school friend who had joined the Army. I came to understand he'd had adventures and, almost on a whim, I decided to go adventuring.

"I applied to join the Army and, soon after, found myself at Mons Officer Cadet School in Aldershot. Mons was an establishment designed to turn out young officers in the minimum training time. The end product tended to be a bit rough at the edges, and after a mere six months, I was commissioned, a Second Lieutenant, Royal Signals. Two weeks later, I arrived in Germany.

"The early years were a very steep learning curve, but I was fortunate in having excellent senior NCOs who were kind and effective mentors. I had initially planned to spend three years in the Army and then to return to a career with prospects into the future. But, after two years, I was recommended for a Regular, that is to say a full-career, commission.

"For five years, I was a Cold War Warrior, based in Germany, but taking part in training in Norway and the Baltic, and as far south as North Africa.

"After five years, I'd had enough of Germany and so I volunteered for a posting to the Middle East. Soon after, I arrived in Aden. It was the last year of the Aden Emergency, a demanding year. My quarters were mortared on the night of my arrival. No casualties, but a lot of excitement.

"My abiding memory of Aden is the ever-present confusion – because there were two nationalist organisations fighting for independence, NLF and FLOSY. They were fighting the British – who, by the way, had already set a date for independence, but they were fighting us anyway – and they were also fighting amongst themselves. So it was confusing and there were many, many deaths.

"On 20th June 1967, due to a misunderstanding, a mutiny in an element of the South Arabian Armed Forces led to the indiscriminate shooting of a party of British soldiers, who were on their way back to barracks from range practice.

"Later that day, there was an ambush by the armed element of the Aden Police on a group consisting of the advance party of the Argyll and Sutherland Highlanders and the rear party of the Royal Northumberland Fusiliers – that is to say, the Royal Northumberland Fusiliers were leaving to be replaced by the Argylls. The group was heading into the district of Crater, as was standard procedure during heightened threat levels, to set up a forward headquarters, in a police station. There were no survivors.

"There was a smaller incident with a few fatalities in Khormaksar. Ten days later, at a funeral at the military cemetery at Silent Valley in Little Aden, we buried twenty-seven soldiers.

"I represented my regiment at the funeral and remember placing a wreath on the grave of a seventeen year old infantryman. Soon afterwards, my unit was attacked in barracks. A young Arab threw a grenade over the perimeter wire, killing one of my soldiers and seriously wounding others.

"The process of setting up a government, to be in place when the British authorities withdrew from Aden, crawled on.

"Finally, the British left in early December 1967. However, there were approximately four hundred and fifty citizens of British and other friendly nations who remained in Aden. There was concern that they could be targets in an uprising, as there was no stable government in the new state – The People's Democratic Republic of South Yemen.

"As a contingency, the British government ordered the Royal Navy to maintain a taskforce offshore to effect a rapid evacuation, backed by a strong amphibious force. There was a requirement for a communication link between the newly established British Embassy in Aden and the taskforce. I was selected to command the small group of Royal Signals personnel, tasked with maintaining that link. We became (non-uniformed) embassy staff. I'm going back fifty years, here.

"So, along with nine other soldiers, I watched the last Royal Air Force plane fly from Aden, and saw the ships of the Royal Navy sail out of Aden Harbour for the last time.

"Ten weeks later, the situation was deemed to be stable and my team and I left Aden in ones and twos, under various guises. I was the last out. We flew out in a Royal Air Force transport aircraft to Bahrain, carrying all our equipment.

"I attended a couple of courses and learnt Arabic, and during the first of my courses, I met Diane. I met her on the way to a blind date (with someone else). We had a long letter-writing relationship. Occasionally, I telephoned her from the Gulf – by now, I had returned to the Middle East, on loan from the British Army to the Army of Abu Dhabi – but I telephoned Diane over a whistly, crackly radio link, when I could. Satellites hadn't arrived yet. The satellite system only appeared about halfway through my time in Abu Dhabi and the time lag on telephone calls made a sensible conversation next to impossible.

"Anyway, living in the Gulf at that time was another adventure. There were almost no roads. Occasionally, I used to go and see a colleague, who was doing a similar job to mine, in Muscat. It would take the best part of two days to drive from Abu Dhabi to Muscat. Now, there's a multi-lane highway.

"I was in Abu Dhabi for a little under two years. I had a brother officer in Abu Dhabi who decided he would drive home. So, we drove from Abu Dhabi to Dubai, took a ferry over to Bandar Abbas in southern Iran, drove up through Iran and eventually crossed into Turkey. We did all this in an Austin 1300. We arrived in Istanbul in the midst of a major cholera outbreak and all the neighbouring countries had sealed their borders. We could go no further. My friend took the ferry from Istanbul to Marseille, but I wanted to get home in a hurry so I flew to London.

"After a few weeks' leave, during which, I proposed to Diane (she accepted), I moved to my next posting with the Guards Armoured Brigade in Germany. And then, at long last, there was a UK posting to Catterick in North Yorkshire. For two years, I drove a desk as a Junior Staff Officer. And our son, Matthew was born, which was the high point of those two years.

"I then had my first tour of Northern Ireland, unaccompanied, for eight months. It was an interesting time, working twelve hours on, twelve hours off, with few breaks and a few adventures.

"After that, I had another short tour as a Staff Officer, based in Bulford Camp, but training all over northern Europe. I was then rewarded with a posting to Berlin.

"For two years, we lived with the Wall. I had interesting forays into Potsdam, over the Glienicke Bridge, which is the Bridge of Spies. We had a detachment, based in Potsdam, surrounded by the East German Army. I also earned the distinction of installing a television for 'The Prisoner', Rudolf Hess, in Spandau Prison. The Allied Commandants, in a rare gesture of generosity, decided that 'The Prisoner', as he was known, should be able to watch the World Cup. I was tuning the set in a spare cell – there were many spare cells – and a voice behind me asked if there was any space in the grandstand. I received no thanks from 'The Prisoner'. In fact, he told me that he had seen a demonstration of colour television in Berlin, in 1938.

"After Berlin, I went back to Northern Ireland. This time, for two years, with the family. They were an unexpectedly happy two years, despite the odd explosion nearby. We lived in comfortable barracks. Matthew attended a local primary school. The only Army brat in his class, he had a personal armed escort to accompany him to and from the school gate. This procedure, he considered absolutely normal. He'd been to kindergarten in Berlin, but started primary school with an armed escort.

"Next, it was time to become a Whitehall Warrior. Comes to all of us. I had two enjoyable and productive years at the Ministry of Defence. It was the first time that I was living outside the 24-hour-a-day military environment. Diane and I bought our first house, just outside Brighton, and I became a commuter, going to work in a suit, for the first time.

"Then, I went to Hong Kong to join the Gurkhas or, more correctly, the Queen's Gurkha Signals. Initially, my role was in operational planning. After twelve months, the Regimental Colonel invited me to extend my time in Hong Kong and take command of the Gurkha Signal Squadron based in Kowloon. These were two really happy, enjoyable and productive years, serving with Nepalese soldiers, who were both professional and consistently amusing.

"Fun was very important because so many were separated from their families, the days needed to be filled with distraction.

"I had three years in total in Hong Kong. By this point, Matthew was in secondary education back in the United Kingdom and flew out to Hong Kong three times a year. During his stays in Hong Kong, he was adopted by my soldiers and was also the object of many curry experiments.

"Back to the United Kingdom. I was posted to East Yorkshire to command a signals school, producing signallers for the logistic and support areas of the Army. Perhaps the most stable three years of my military career, I was in a job that was governed by timetables and targets, with a good degree of autonomy.

"I was heading towards the time when I would complete my military career when, unexpectedly, after three years in East Yorkshire, I received an unusual appointment as the assistant defence attaché in Seoul, with an additional, concurrent job as the United Kingdom liaison officer to the United Nations Military Armistice Commission in Korea. (The longest job title of my career!)

"The latter job demanded more hours than the former. I did not, nor was I required to, master the Korean language. The job entailed many hours in protracted discussions among the Allies and with the 'North Side' – the North Koreans and the Chinese People's Army.

"Matthew was still at school in Sussex. Meanwhile, Diane and I lived in a less-fashionable district in Seoul, surrounded by a mixture of embassies and – a wide range of other establishments which offered entertainment to the nearby United States Army Garrison.

"The meetings at Panmunjom were fascinating, in that, the full plenary sessions of the Military Armistice Commission would be called at the request of the North Koreans, who would never provide an agenda. So, the South Side would formulate a game plan to cover all eventualities.

"On one occasion, the draft game plan was delivered to our house late in the evening, ready for a pre-meeting conference early the following morning. Diane and I sat up in bed, and read through the prepared variety of statements, making amendments where we considered the language perhaps too harsh or inexact.

"The following morning, some of our suggested amendments were accepted at the preparatory meeting of the United Nations group and that evening, as we watched a report of the full meeting on local television, Diane was amused when she heard her 'sentence' being delivered by a senior United States General.

"The majority of the other meetings there involved lower ranking officers addressing more mundane subjects, such as the security of the conference area. These meetings were held behind closed doors, at a comparatively junior level, with more realistic targets. Often, at the end of these meetings, we had drinks with our opposite numbers from North Korea and China. One of the specialities offered by the North Side was a rice-based spirit called Soju. Occasionally, the drink was enhanced by the inclusion of a small viper, which had been placed in the bottle, alive, and had subsequently drowned. It gave the drink some bite.

"At the outset of my time in Korea, I was fascinated by the history of the Korean War. I was able to find plenty of time to walk over the battlefields of that War, particularly those to the north of Seoul and close to the North-South border. I was soon running small tours for anyone who was interested and wanted to appreciate the challenges of fighting in that terrain. This was my first taste of battlefield guiding.

"Each year, in April, there would be a ceremony to mark the anniversary of the Battle of the Imjin, fought by the British Army in 1951. In particular, the exploits of the Gloucestershire Regiment, which was overrun, fighting a rearguard action. I was privileged to meet many veterans including General Anthony Farrar-Hockley, who had fought at the Battle of the Imjin, and was taken into captivity.

"The General had been appointed as the official British historian of the Korean War, and had already completed part one of his history before I arrived in Korea. When I met him, he was in the process of writing the second, and final, part of the history, and I became his bag-carrier when he visited Korea for research.

"During my own research and wanderings, I made a number of friends in the Republic of Korea Army. About twelve months before I left Korea, I received a call one evening from a young Korean Army Officer who told me that his soldiers had come across a skeleton whilst digging a trench on a hill south of the Imjin: this area had been occupied by a company of the Gloucestershire Regiment in their final battle.

"As thirty Gloucestershire soldiers had never been accounted for, I was, naturally, excited. The following day, I went to the site with Diane, Matthew and my Korean driver, Mr. Kim. With the Korean soldiers' help, we started an excavation, and uncovered a complete skeleton.

"The following day, we returned to the site with an American colleague who was the United States Army's official historian in Korea. He was equipped, more professionally than we, with a metal detector. We recovered the skeleton, which had been buried in a trench, which was no doubt dug and occupied by the Gloucesters. In the base of the trench, we found a large quantity of ammunition and personal effects, such as a razor, fountain pen, toothbrush, but no weapon. We were hoping to find an I.D. tag. With the last ping of the metal detector, we uncovered a cap badge of the Gloucestershire Regiment.

"We went back to Seoul and handed over the skeleton to the United States Army Mortuary. The officer at the mortuary thought that the remains were more likely Caucasian than Asiatic but could not confirm this. Eventually, the remains were sent to the Central Identification Authority in Hawaii, which is a centre of excellence for forensic examination and holds the records of every American and Allied serviceman lost in the Pacific region for conflicts up to and including the Vietnam War.

"I went to Hawaii. I was invited to visit and the American forces were kind enough to provide a beachside bungalow for my family and me.

"Shortly after my return to the United Kingdom, having finished my time in Seoul, I received formal notification that the skeleton was Asiatic, probably a Chinese soldier, a casualty of the Imjin Battle.

"I was posted to Exeter where – at the time, I couldn't know – I was going to spend the last ten years of my military career. We bought a house three months after we arrived – our twenty-third address during our marriage."

<Me: Twenty-third? I've had two addresses in my life.>

"Twenty-seven years on, we're still here. It's the longest we've lived anywhere.

"I've never absolutely severed my connection with the Army. I retired forty years after enlisting. I took a year off, became a battlefield guide and have been taking servicemen, from recruits to senior officers, to the battlefields of north-west Europe ever since. In this capacity, I meet – probably several hundred –servicemen every year."

Keith

"MY FIRST INSTRUCTION to Naval service was this: I was to present myself at an RN Office in London. Then, with a group of other recruits, I was to catch a train at Paddington to go to Corsham in Wiltshire, known as HMS Royal Arthur.

"Once there, we were allocated huts, fed, and told to settle down. The big shock in the morning was being awoken by a bugle, blowing Reveille, as a Petty Officer walked through the central corridor, shouting. I believe the rest of the day was taken up with various medicals, and also the next day. Out of the original group that had left London, at least half of them were rejected as 'medically unfit'.

"On the third day, we signed on the dotted line, committing ourselves to a period of Service. In 1948, I signed up for seven years with the Fleet, and five in Reserve. Following the ceremony of receiving the King's Shilling, we received our full kit and hammock, and a blanket. The blanket was a utility make but I kept it for over fifty years and it was in general use for most of that time. We were not allowed 'ashore' for a fortnight and our time was filled with various tests and parade ground drill.

"After the required fortnight, we were allowed ashore, so I caught a train from Bath to Beckington to visit Granny Greene, and Mother, who was staying with her. I also remember seeing a couple of friends I had when living there and I was pleased that a girl who was then eighteen recognised me and gave me a hug!

"Three days later, the whole class (twenty-five), left Corsham by train and travelled to Weymouth to join our training ship: an aircraft carrier, HMS Victorious. The ship was one of three known as the Training

Battle Squadron, consisting of two Battleships – Anson and Howe – and Victorious, anchored in the middle of Portland Harbour. The class was taken out to the ship in an MFV, Motor Fishing Vessel and, after some delay, shown to our mess and given a meal. I cannot remember the meal, but I do remember seeing beautiful white bread baked in the on-board bakery. I should explain that because of the shortages caused by the War, rationing was still in force, which included bread. The flour that was used ashore by the bakers was a mixture of various types of grain and/or bran, and because nothing could be wasted, even the sweepings from the floor were included. The bread produced was a dirty grey colour. The flour used on board was obviously the best quality and pure.

"The following weeks were taken up with turning young men, who were wet behind the ears, from civilians into seamen. We learnt how to tie knots, we learnt about anchors and cables, marching, a smattering of navigation, how to sail and row a boat (usually a cutter or whaler), and how to keep ourselves clean, dhobing our clothes. We learnt responsibility.

"On a more personal note, I was made a class leader after a couple of weeks, which meant I had to organise the mess, make certain it was clean, and take charge of the class in the absence of our Instructor. A fairly rough introduction to the new life was being involved at a very early stage in an Admiral's Inspection. Being newcomers, it did not affect us all that much, apart from going to sea in an aircraft carrier in a force nine gale. Despite the fact that the ship was large, it still rolled and pitched, causing many of the class, including me, to be sick.

"My other memory of this time was standing (parading) on the flight deck to enter harbour, and watching a pool of rainwater freezing! The other highlight was sailing to Guernsey to represent the Country and Royal Navy at their liberation ceremonies.

"We arrived during the early evening in a fog and, as I was a duty watchman, I was given the job of sounding a warning bell every minute or so from the quarterdeck, so that other ships would avoid us. I did that during the whole of the first watch, 20.00–23.59! Next day was sunny and I was given the job of cleaning the quarterdeck during the forenoon before going ashore on 'foreign' soil for the very first time.

"On return to Portland, our training continued, until the great day dawned when we would 'pass out' and be the top class. The process gave me some encouragement, as I was second in the class, with pass-out marks in the high eighties, so I felt I was not such a nerd as I thought I was!

"Our training programme was curtailed by three weeks when, as a class, we were sent to Portsmouth on a scheme called 'party bun'. Our job was to de-store ships so they could either be placed in reserve or broken up. I spent some time on a fairly old, three-funnel cruiser called Berwick, which was built in the 1920s. I was then transferred to a Battle Class destroyer, The Saintes, for the rest of the three weeks. During this time, I was living on a light cruiser called HMS Sirius.

"We were then transferred to HMS Excellent, on Whale Island, to complete our training. After summer leave, ten days, I returned to Whale Island to do a three-month gunnery course. As the course did not start for three weeks, I was sent to work in the pig and chicken farm on the island. The gunnery course was completed by November and I was then transferred to Chatham, where I was detailed to be a member of the 'beef boat'. The job entailed loading an MFV with various stores, mainly foodstuffs, and delivering these to the ships moored in the Medway. We then tied up in Sheerness and had lunch. Although rationing was still very much in force, it did not affect us as we took a share of the food we were carrying and so, lived in high style.

"After about four weeks going up and down the Medway in all weathers, my name appeared on the draft board in the barrack drill shed – instructing me to join HMS Corunna when she returned to Chatham. Although I did not think about it at the time, I was to be on the ship for over two years, and during that time, I moved from being an ordinary seaman to a Leading Seaman with six months' seniority.

"I joined the ship, a Battle Class destroyer, just before Christmas and was promptly sent on ten days' Christmas leave. On my return, all the seamen were at work, painting the ship, which took at least a week. In the meantime, I was taken off general duties and became a member of the Gunners Party. I was responsible for 'B' turret – maintaining the outside and ensuring that the inside was always clean and ready for any snap inspection.

"We left Chatham dockyard on a Saturday in late February and sailed up the east coast to meet an aircraft carrier in the Firth of Forth. As we sailed north, the weather got progressively worse, the wind increasing to a full gale, and the ship, rolling and pitching quite violently. During the morning watch on deck, I was sick and miserable. By the evening, when we were rounding the top of Scotland in the Pentland Firth, the weather was so violent that all hands were banned from the upper deck. We found out later that we had made the English newsreels, shown in the cinemas at home, and it illustrated that the sea was so rough that over a third of the ship, from the bows towards the stern, was completely out of the water. No wonder I felt ill!

"However, everything settled down and the ship arrived in Gibraltar three days late. Although it was still March, the weather was sunny and warm. The ship spent a further four weeks in the Mediterranean before returning home for Easter leave and Navy Days. Our next deployment was to be attached to the Mediterranean Fleet for six months, during which we were deployed in Aqaba, Cyprus, Italy, Malta, Egypt and, of course, Gibraltar.

"We returned home in late August, went on fourteen days' leave, rejoined the ship and then, spent the next two months or so sailing between Portland, Scotland and Northern Ireland.

"During the whole time, we seemed to be in force nine gales, with wind and tides so strong that the mooring wires (two and a half inches thick) were parting like pieces of string. At one time, when we were attempting to tie-up at an oiling jetty, all of the mooring wires parted, forcing us to use the towing wire (four and a half inches thick) and hurricane hawsers (a mixture of heavy wire and six inch rope that was used as a spring).

"In the fullness of time, we returned to Chatham. Christmas leave was granted to one watch, so the remaining crew carried on with normal harbour routine until it was their turn for leave.

"January 1949 saw the ship leaving port to spend the spring in the Mediterranean, exercising with the Med Fleet. At one time, the whole of the Home and Mediterranean Fleet combined and, as far as the eye could see, there were ships of all shapes and sizes, covering a very large area of the sea. The highlight of this was that it was the last time four Battleships – Vanguard, King George V, Anson and Howe – were at sea together. I believe that three of them were placed in reserve when they arrived home and the fourth, Vanguard, continued her life before she was placed in reserve and eventually scrapped.

"By this time, I had decided that I should be paid more and perhaps tell other people what to do instead of being a most people's beck and call. I requested to sit the board (exam) for Leading Seaman, and so commenced three or four months of reading nothing but the Seamanship manual. At the same time, my job on the ship was changed to that of an officer's servant. That meant he had to be woken with tea in the morning, his cabin cleaned, his washing and ironing done. As well as this, there was duty night work in the wardroom. This suited me very well as it gave me more time to study for the approaching board.

"In the meantime, the Home Fleet had commenced the Summer Cruise, based in Portland Harbour. This meant we would go out on exercises during the week and visit either home ports or resorts over the weekends to 'show the Flag'.

"The first resort we visited was Sidmouth, anchoring about half a mile off shore, opposite the sailing club. On Saturday, the ship was open to visitors, so everyone was on their best behaviour. I went ashore on Sunday, and visited Exmouth to call on an old friend and neighbour of my parents. I remember it was a fairly pleasant occasion, as the family were on the beach and it was nice to relax and be ashore without pressure.

"Unfortunately, when I got back to Sidmouth, we were unable to return to the ship because the waves had increased in height and the ship's boat was unable to come inshore. So, the night was spent walking around the town, to the station and back, and looking at Jacob's Ladder. The night eventually passed, the sea had gone down, so the ship's boat was able to come in and return us to the ship.

"The following weekend, we visited the Scilly Isles and, although we were able to go ashore and spend some time wandering around, we were recalled on board as the wind and swell had increased and the ship was dragging the anchor. After several attempts to re-anchor, the Captain gave up and the ship moved to Mounts Bay, where we successfully 'dropped the hook'.

"Our next move was up to Rosyth. Those of us who were waiting for the Leading Seamen's Board were told it would be held in a few days' time: a Monday morning. We were given the test jobs – making a 'bollard strop' in two and a half inch wire, and producing some 'tiddly' work in sisal rope. These jobs would have to be done on board within the two days, and the only place to carry out such work was in the tiller flat.

"I started work on Sunday at about midday, and completed the task at about 21.30. I thought: a good night's sleep, up early, shower, put on my newly pressed number threes, and all set. Rubbish. A Scottish candidate had returned off shore at about the time I had finished and he had not thought about the splicing. He got changed and between us, we finished his jobs at about five in the morning. The only consolation was that I was able to have a peaceful, hot shower and take my time shaving. I received the best news the next day from the Captain: I had passed with a good result.

"We left Rosyth and sailed to Lossiemouth. The rest of the 4th Destroyer Squadron was already there. Unfortunately, we lost a sub-Lieutenant who had tried to swim from another ship back to Corunna and had drowned. We delayed our departure for two days while the ship's boat carried out a thorough search of the Loch. Eventually, the ship sailed, due north, to Malmö in Sweden, and then, further north to Trondheim. I think that's the only time I have been that far north, when it was continual daylight.

"We sailed south again, this time between the mainland and off islands, where we were amazed to see so many Norwegian flags outside the houses. The Norwegians were, in turn, amazed to see us in a fairly small destroyer, following an aircraft carrier which was so large, it appeared to touch both sides of the cliffs at once.

"After the summer leave, we left Chatham and sailed down the Channel to Portland, where we were based for about three weeks, exercising AS-DICs in the Portland Races and carrying out main armament shoots, before sailing further down the Channel to Plymouth. Our duties there were to be the crash boat to an aircraft carrier, which was training pilots in night flying and landings.

"Unfortunately, they advanced the time of the flights every night which meant the same part of the watch, first port, were up for three nights getting the ship underway, manning the crash boat, and then anchoring the ship on return to harbour. I know this to be true because I was in the first part of the port watch.

"However, at the end of the week, we left Plymouth and sailed down to Gibraltar. It was unfortunate that we hit a force nine gale, which continued for most of the way. From Gib, we went further down, passing the Canary Islands to the Cape Verde Islands. How things change in a short time! As the sea was calm, I saw flying fish for the first time, and we were able to keep the morning watch on deck in a pair of shorts and warm sunshine.

"On arrival off the Cape Verde Islands, we had to paint the ship. This involved dangling over the side of the ship on two pieces of rope which were holding a 'stage' – a plank with a cross-piece of timber at either end. We were lowered from this to paint the side of the ship. There were only two drawbacks: the sea was shark-infested, and, at one point, while the ship was taking on fuel, a pipe burst, spilling fuel over the paintwork and the deck. All painting stopped while the mess was cleaned up and then the damaged part had to be repainted.

"During this time, we were working tropical routine, starting at 04.00 and finishing at midday. But on that particular day, we were working for fifteen hours solidly.

"After the Cape Verde Islands, we proceeded to Casablanca and then back to Gibraltar where, on the day we were leaving for home (late November 1950), I was rated Leading Seaman and was then told I was in charge of the afternoon watch.

"Being promoted was a peculiar experience because, during the previous weeks, I had to prove that I was ready for advancement by being the first to jump to any job, to show how keen I was, and the first to volunteer. Once promoted, I had to learn to step back and watch other people carry out the jobs that I had been doing the day before, and to start with, that was quite difficult. The big advantage was that, although I had the afternoon watch, when we were also 'crash boat' to the Canadian Carrier, Magnificent, I was excused the middle watch because my opposite number had offered to do it. In fact, for the four days' sailing between Gibraltar and Chatham, I did not do a night watch.

"However, I was in charge of the anchor watch on the forecastle from Sheerness to Chatham Dockyard. The days on Corunna were numbered, as two years spent on any ship was considered to be a 'commission'. I eventually left her in late January 1951, and was drafted to the Chatham Barracks to complete a second-class gunnery course. Having completed the course, also a week's gas and firefighting course, I had to report sick, and remained in the sick bay for some three months.

"The highlight of my time in the Barracks was that Lilian was working in an office situated in the Drill Shed and I could meet her as she was walking to the WRENS quarters for lunch. We occasionally went out together, played table tennis and generally chatted about various friends, etc. Eventually, Lilian was drafted to the Mercury in Hampshire and, after Christmas leave, I was drafted to the Tyne, to serve in the Reserve Fleet in Malta. However, before I went, Lilian and I met in London and spent the weekend together, staying in the Union Jack Club, which resembled a doss house.

"It was about this time that King George died. Lilian queued for hours to see the King, lying in state, in Westminster Hall, guarded by high-ranking officers from the three services.

"When we said goodbye on Waterloo Station, neither of us realised that it would be just over four years until we met again. What a waste of time!!

"Following my return to Chatham, I was doing odd jobs. On the day of the King's funeral, I was sent down to Dover with two seamen, to escort a deserter back to Chatham. Another day, I was responsible for escorting another miscreant to Portsmouth Barracks, to serve his sixty-day sentence in their cells. Not a very pleasant experience!

"This way of life continued until my draft came up. I was to go to London, stay in the deep shelters in the Tottenham Court Road overnight and, with at least forty other draftees, fly to Malta the next day: February 29th 1952.

"It was the first time I had been in an aircraft, so I managed to secure a window seat. The flight time was all day. The plane landed at Nice airport for refuelling, and at Luqa airport in Malta at about 18.30. After the usual hanging around for baggage, I eventually joined my ship, HMS Tyne, at about seven thirty in the evening.

"The ship's routine was a bit of a shock as 'call the hands' was 05.45, scrub decks at 06.15, breakfast at 07.15, 'both watches' at 08.15. As a member of the Reserve Fleet, I had to catch a boat to the particular reserve ships I was detailed to work on. I found the situation very boring, as there wasn't a lot to do because the reserve ships did not move and, with the attention paid to them, only needed superficial maintenance.

"Not long after I had joined the Tyne, polio was diagnosed in one of the crew members. This meant that the ship was quarantined. After a few weeks, it was decided that all the Reserve Fleet personnel should be sent to Fort Rikazoli, a very old fort, sited at the entrance of Grand Harbour, and be transported daily to Lazaretto Creek, where the Reserve Fleet was secured.

"After a few weeks, the polio cycle had been broken, so everything returned to normal. At about this time, my daily routine was changed and I was put in charge of a boat, two crew, and started a period of twenty-four hours on duty, twenty-four hours off. This also meant wearing white uniforms during the summer and full blues in the winter. There was also a lot more washing (dhobing) of clothes, full uniforms, etc.

"The advantages were few, except that when I was in the boat, I was the boss, and together with the crew, we cleaned the boat from bow to stern until it gleamed white and all of us were very proud of our achievements.

"As life was very much routine, I decided it was time that I should look for some advancement, so I requested to be included in the next Petty Officer's board. The request was granted so, for the foreseeable future, my only reading was the Seamanship manual, as the date of a board could be sprung at a day's notice.

"Unfortunately, when the day came, my name was not included on the list of applicants to take the board and I had to return to my ship, very disappointed and upset. However, after a formal enquiry, I had to attend the 'Captain's Request Men', and was assured that a board would be convened within fourteen days, and that my name would be on the top of the list. Fifteen days later, I was told that I had passed for Petty Officer, with a very respectable mark and, although it was November, my pass was backdated to June. Hooray!!

"During the rest of the year, and into spring of the following year, every day followed a routine: either watch-keeping on boats or doing various jobs within the Reserve Fleet. However, all this came to an end at the end of May 1953, when I was told that a group of sailors and I would be transferred to the Fort Duquesne Navy supply ship, as Naval Armed

Party, for at least six weeks. We would be based in Lake Timsah, off Ismailia.

"My job, with another Leading Seaman, was to run a boat into Ismailia and to carry out patrols around the ship, looking for frogmen. Both crews changed every twenty-four hours, so during our free period, we either went swimming or sailing and, in the evening, went ashore. Because the Egyptians did not like us, shore time was limited to being picked up in an Army bus and taken to the nearest military camp, Fort Moasca Garrison, where there was a cinema and bar. I went to the cinema once as the film being shown was *The Cruel Sea*, which we all enjoyed.

"We were able to listen to parts of the Coronation ceremony on the radio, but as I was the duty coxswain from midday, I missed most of it. I could not help comparing the difference between the reported June weather in London, which was cold and wet, to the very warm weather we were used to.

"On Coronation Day, we experienced was a very hot, sunny day, with a cloudless sky, no wind, and a temperature between 85 and 90 degrees. Bliss! Towards the middle of July, the Naval Party was transferred to HMS Ranpura in Port Said, and returned to Malta.

"On arrival on my old ship, I found that I had been assigned to a different mess deck, much smaller than the one I had been in before, and only containing ten other people. Also, my job, which I was doing only eight weeks before, was no longer available – which, in some ways, I was delighted to learn.

"However, my time of leisure did not materialise as I was detailed with two 'hands' to produce new mooring wires for the ships of the Reserve Fleet. This meant splicing 'soft eyes' in two and a half inch wire. The wire was made up of seven 'strands' which, during the splicing, would be 'tucked' three times around the wire and then, reduced by cutting out two of the thin strands over the last three tucks, thus finishing with a tapered splice. The whole lot was then covered in spun yarn. The mooring wire was finished in four days, and then, I had the job of checking and re-rigging the various small boats carried by the minelayers and, having completed the work, taking them on trial, half a day sailing, and making any adjustments that were required. At the time, I thought it was a fantastic way to earn my living, doing what some people were paying hundreds of pounds to do on holiday.

"Like all good things, the job came to an end just about the same time as I was drafted to a destroyer, HMS Chequers.

"This was like a new chapter in my life. It was the first time I had been the senior Leading Seaman on the forecastle, so I spent the first couple of weeks understudying the ways things were done and who did what. Life was settling down again when the new 'Watch & Quarter' bill was posted and, to my horror, I saw that I was watch-keeping on the ship's boat. Unfortunately, my pleas to the First Lieutenant to be moved to another position met with no success. However, the Leading Seaman who had been named as the Captain's Coxswain did not want the job so, with permission, we swapped. The only drawback, if there was one, was getting up before the rest of the crew and ensuring the boat was 'tiddly' before picking up the Captain. And, of course, wearing whites all day. Despite these minor set backs, I thoroughly enjoyed the job.

"After a couple of weeks in the job, a newer, faster boat was delivered to the ship. The Captain's old boat became the ship's boat, and the old ship's boat was returned to the dockyard. At the same time, the ship was due to sail to Port Said for a two month stay as guard boat, so arrangements were made, with the help of a shipwright, that the new boat would be stripped of paint and repainted with a new colour. The deck would be stained and varnished, and all the 'brightwork' given an extra polish.

"We left Sliema early one morning to sail to Port Said. En route, the ship was stopped during the 'Dog Watches' for the off duty crew to go swimming – a fantastic experience as the water was very blue, very deep and unbelievably warm. I should add, there was always one person keeping an eye on the swimmers in case of any difficulties. On arrival in port, the ship docked, stern to the wall, and all boats were dropped off. There was little to do in Egypt, as we were not allowed ashore because of the animosity shown to us by everyone apart from the traders, who would have welcomed us with open arms! However, there was an inter-mess 'deck hockey' competition, played on the concrete jetty, the final being played between the wardroom and my mess. During the final, I made a fairly hard and rough contact with the engineer officer by missing the puck and hitting him very hard on his ankle. I did apologise; he took it in good sport and told me not to worry, but for the rest of the game, I was a marked man and he succeeded in getting his revenge! At the end, we won the match and everyone shook hands. In the mean-time, the Captain's new boat was progressing.

"We had got as far as painting the white area, so we called up to the wireless office for a weather report, which was favourable. And so, 'Chippy' and I spent the next hour and a half painting white enamel paint on the superstructure and finished just as the sun was setting. It was a little worrying that some black clouds were approaching, but there was nothing we could do about it, so we went back on board for the evening meal.

"Next morning, I looked at the boat, which resembled a piece of coarse sandpaper. Unfortunately, the weather forecast had been wrong. There had been a gale overnight which had blown fresh sand all over our work. During the day, we cleared everything off, washed it and repainted, successfully this time.

"Once the boat had been finished, the Captain used it to visit other ships and, at one time, took a trip down the canal in an American Destroyer. He had to be picked up on the return trip while the ship he had been on kept moving. I found it difficult to match the speed of the larger ship on such a small boat. Fortunately, he was able to board the boat without any mishap!

"Another time, when I was crossing the harbour, there was a small Egyptian 'fleet' coming the other way. I suddenly realised that on board the Egyptian boats was General Naguib and his entourage so, in line with protocol, I stopped the boat, called the crew to 'attention' and saluted. He returned my salute, smiled and gave us a wave!

"Our time in Port Said was coming to an end. The time in harbour had been fairly busy. The ship had been painted from top to bottom, and generally got ready for an Admiral's Inspection. The decision was made that we would go to sea for one day and carry out the scheduled shoot, main armament.

"When we left harbour, the weather was changing from the normal warm and still days to a fairly brisk wind and cloud. As far as I am aware, the shoot was successful, except for 'B' gun, which misfired. There is a set routine for a misfire where the gun-captain, on orders from the gunnery officer, presses a 'clear gun push' which, hopefully, fires the offending shell. Unfortunately for the gun-captain, his head was in the way of the breech, so when the gun fired, it recoiled and the breech block opened sideways, hitting the captain in the face. What none of the crew realised was that the accident was the start of a run of accidents and bad luck that would continue to affect the ship for many weeks to come. More of that later...

"The ship left Port Said in the early morning, heading west. We made good time during the day, despite a rising wind from the west and we fully expected to reach Malta in the normal three days. Unfortunately, during the night, we hit some really bad weather, with rising seas and a full gale blowing up to force 10-11, known locally as the Gregale. For the only time during my period of service, the ship was forced into the wind, with just enough speed to keep the 'bows' facing the weather.

"For the next couple of days, we were in this position. The ship was driven backwards, we lost the crew's boat, smashed from the davits. We lost the 'skimmer' and the dingy, which had been bolted to the iron deck with two-inch bolts, and also a washdeck locker that had been welded to the ship's superstructure.

"Those of the crew who lived aft stayed there, and those of us forward carried out our duties by keeping on the leeward side of the bridge superstructure. We eventually made Malta in six and a half days, rather battered. As we were preparing the ship for an Admiral's Inspection, we only had the weekend in harbour. The future programme was to spend several days at sea, carrying out various exercises and returning to Sliema at night. That's when a series of accidents occurred.

"The first was this: a young, ordinary seaman was fetching a bucket of hot water from the galley at the same time as the Chief GI. Unfortunately, the GI's bucket slipped and splashed the OD with very hot water. The OD finished up in the sickbay.

"Next day, whilst at sea, a fire was reported in number one boiler room. Big emergency, the boiler room was more or less filled with foam, and the fire put out. I believe it took the stokers over a week to clean up the mess. Those of the upper deck thought it was quite funny.

"The next day, we were carrying out a gunnery exercise with all guns. The Director was sited above the bridge and resembled a large round glasshouse with two large radar nacelles either side. All the main armament was controlled from the Director post, with a crew of five trained specialists. From my position, I controlled all the guns' elevation. My opposite number was the trainer, who was responsible for the various bearings. There was also another fantastic piece of equipment in a compartment below that worked out all the various adjustments needed – for ship's speed, enemy's speed, wind speed, cordite temperature, etc. When the fire gong sounded, I pulled the trigger and fired all the main armament. What power!

"When we had finished the shoot, another exercise was to take place and only needed one person in the Director, which could be controlled by a joystick, and that was me. Unfortunately, when I closed the sliding door, which was made of quarter inch steel, the small finger of my right hand was in the way and the door ripped out the left side of the nail. It still grows oddly.

"Because of my problem, I was excused duty for the rest of the day and arrangements were made for me to see a doctor on another ship later on. As we were entering Sliema Creek in the evening, we lost all steam in the boiler room at the most critical time possible. The ship was in the middle of a turn with the bows hanging over the shore. I understand a general call for help was sent out. A frigate, entering Grand Harbour, turned round, and a minesweeper slipped her cable in her hurry to help us. Fortunately, the problem was solved very quickly, and we proceeded up the Creek in an orderly fashion.

"For my part, I attended the Medical Guard on the Daring, the first of its class of destroyers. Compared to the destroyer I was on, it was like walking onto a large cruiser. Most disconcerting! The doctor could not offer much help either. After leaving the doctor, I went to the cinema on Manoel Island, met up with some of my old friends from Lofoten, and saw the film *Blackbeard*.

"In the fullness of time, the Admiral's Inspection took place: Divisions, Messdeck Inspection and General Drills. The drills could be anything. I was part of a party securing a 'boom' – a length of wood, which was extended from the ship's side for an electrician to walk out onto and boil an electric kettle. To carry out this exercise, we had to erect and secure 'sheerlegs' – a type of lifting device, made of wood and rope, and using a block and tackle. I remember we got the boom in position just before we ran out of time. I think the electrician was very relieved!

"At the end of the evening, I was standing on the bows of the Captain's boat, when a seaman fell from the upper deck into the sea directly in front of me. Being a hero, I dived in to support him (dressed in my blue suit) – at the same time as the Captain required his boat. Panic. I had to get back inboard, strip off my wet blues, wipe down and clean my uniform, and get back quickly. By this time, the Captain's boat had been piped at least three times. I had to take the grumpy Captain to Msida. Fortunately, he accepted my explanation.

"After this episode, we resumed our normal routine, but towards December, we were a part of a NATO submarine hunting group, controlled by a French Admiral. Unfortunately, it did not start well as the Admiral said it was too rough for his ships. The Captain, being the senior British Officer, replied that he was taking the RN ships to sea, and would report directly to NATO HQ. It was quite amazing how quickly the remainder of the taskforce slipped their buoys. We spent a week chasing submarines before docking in Marseille, where most of the French sailors were going on Christmas leave.

"I was allowed ashore with the Boy Seamen as I was their mess 'Killick', Leading Seaman. We returned to Malta for Christmas and, on Christmas Day, the Captain offered the use of his boat to the other Flotilla Captains. We had a fairly busy morning when the weather was decidedly not Mediterranean, blowing a gale with rain. The rest of the day passed quietly enough, relaxing in the mess, warm and content. The usual routine continued the next day. Christmas only lasts one day in the Navy. The Captain only used his boat once, there and back from Pieta, so I finished at about three o'clock on Boxing Day.

"After the New Year, 1954, I was rated Petty Officer, so had the pleasure of moving from my mess to the Petty Officers' mess, not having to fight my way to the bathroom, and not living in such cramped conditions. It was rather peculiar, as most of the Petty Officers were married, so at 16.00, there was a mass exodus of all the married men, going ashore to see their wives, leaving only four of us in the mess. However, when at sea, things were different. Everyone was aboard, and the available room in the mess was somewhat cramped.

"The position of the mess on the ship was forward of the Wardroom, with 'B' gun on top of us and 'A' gun just forward. There were two doors from the upper deck which were supposed to be watertight. Unfortunately, during the rough weather, they failed miserably! Our other problem was 'B' gun sitting overhead. When it was fired, everything in the mess 'took wings' and we spent some time having a good clean up! Despite these minor setbacks, it was a very happy time and, as far as I was concerned, it was one of the best times I had in the Royal Navy.

"At the beginning of 1954, the Mediterranean Fleet started to carry out exercises designed to impress not only the Queen (who was due in Malta later that year), but every Naval Attaché and visiting Officer in Malta. The C in C had decided that the whole fleet should meet the Royal Yacht at sea, and carry out high speed manoeuvres, with the destroyers passing the Yacht at one cable's length, at thirty-four knots."

<Me: Just looked it up for those of us who don't know the sea. A knot is a unit of speed equal to one nautical mile an hour. One knot, when compared to land speed is around 1.15mph. So, when the destroyers

were doing 34 knots, as they were passing the Royal Yacht, they were going at what I would understand as close to 40mph.>

"At the time, Prince Charles, who was still a child, was aboard the Yacht. He spoke to me about it fifty years later when I was awarded my MBE at Buckingham Palace, so it must have been impressive.

"I think we carried out the full exercise at least four times, as well as resuming our normal training schedule, before being detached to spend some time on the French Riviera, eventually arriving at Cannes for their celebration of the Entente Cordiale. To assist with the celebration, we carried a full Royal Marine Band, who went ashore every evening 'Beating the Retreat', and paraded on the jetty every morning for the ceremonial 'Hoisting the Colours'. It was noticeable that the music the band played in the morning was more muted than at night due, we suspected, to the fact that half the band were suffering from hangovers.

"As the Captain's boat was not required, we were tied up to a jetty. I had a fairly easy time, except for one afternoon, when I was the only seaman Petty Officer on board, and was in charge of a working party which was black-leading and polishing the iron deck. It was the policy of all Naval ships, especially in harbour, that they should be presented as a shining example to the outside world so, at any opportunity, paint-work was washed, and brightwork and the iron deck was polished.

"During the rest of our stay in Cannes, which was Whitsun, we went ashore on the beach in the afternoon. We came back on board at about six o'clock, had our evening meal, and went ashore again around nine o'clock, returning sometime in the early hours of the morning.

"One of the reasons we were so late was that, on the way back to the ship, we passed a local market. Although, it was very early, the produce from the local farms, etc. was being unloaded and it was an education to see large baskets, filled with various produce. Most impressive were the baskets of carnations and soft fruit. Like all good things, our visit to Cannes finished, and we left at about ten in the morning, with the local populace waving. As it was Whit Monday, the ship 'closed down' apart from the duty watches, and it was estimated that the remainder of the ship's company, including the Captain, was asleep by eleven o'clock!

"After our manoeuvres, we were due to greet the Queen and the Royal Yacht. The great day dawned. A typical Mediterranean summer's day, calm dark blue sea, and a beautiful cloudless sky. As we approached the Royal Yacht, the four escorting minesweepers carried out a ninety-degree turn, leaving plenty of room for the remainder of the fleet to pass the Yacht at great speed. Our signalmen on the bridge were having to work extremely hard, as it appeared all the signal halyards were in full use and the signal bridge deck was filled with used flags. Eventually, the fleet settled down in their steaming positions, and Chequers had the honour of escorting the Royal Yacht towards Malta.

"The Queen remained in Malta for four days, and then left to visit Gozo. Although the weather was fine, the wind had increased to nearly a full gale. Chequers was ahead of the Royal Yacht, and we were all surprised at how much it was pitching. It appeared to be making heavy weather of the conditions. However, we soon reached Gozo, stayed for a few hours, and then sailed for Gibraltar. The escort consisted of one cruiser and three destroyers. All apart from Chequers were heading home and paying off. As Chequers was staying in the Med, she would be replaced by another home fleet destroyer. The local population welcomed the Queen with open arms, and right on the top of the 'Rock', there was a very large and floodlit 'EIIR', pointing directly towards Spain. The Yacht was secured to an outer jetty. There was some concern that Spanish frogmen may try and fix a limpet mine below her water line, so it was decided that she would have to be guarded from her outboard side.

"Unfortunately, the only boat available was the Captain's, so we had to dress in our best suits and patrol the starboard side of the yacht. Most of the time, it was boring. We would start the engine, steer towards the yacht's bows, shut the engine down and drift towards the stern. The only time that it became more interesting was when we watched the Queen performing an Investiture on the Quarterdeck. Later in the day, the yacht sailed and, as she was passing the entrance, signalled to Chequers – 'Splice The Main Brace' – that cheered everyone up!"

<Me: In case it needs saying: 'Splice the mainbrace' is a Naval term which means that the crew are permitted to have a drink.>

"We stayed in Gibraltar for a few days and, during this time, an invitation was received by the Chiefs and Petty Officers from the Garrison's Sergeants' Mess to attend a social evening. As two of us were junior, it was *suggested* that we should attend, so Ron and I decided that, before we joined the party, we would have a couple of drinks in what was known as the Garrison. We were surprised when arriving in the bar, the ship's Coxswain and Chief GI were already there, and were also attending the same 'do'.

"In the end, it turned out to be a good evening, everyone was really friendly and made sure we were not ignored. One of the highlights of the event was the big draw, which I won. Imagine my dismay when I was presented with a china cake stand, which, after some explaining and persuasion, I managed to get substituted with a bottle of beer. However, the Sergeant Major was unhappy with the arrangement and presented me with a bottle of whisky instead.

"Next day, we returned to Malta and once again started to prepare for the Admiral's Inspection, as well as carrying out normal routine and 'showing the Flag' at various places, such as the Greek Islands and Italy. One more memorable occasion was being in Naples. A fairly large group of Petty Officers went ashore en-masse and we appeared to have trouble in finding somewhere to eat. In the end, we bought some ham, butter, and long loaves. We then went to a back street bar, ordered carafes of wine straight from the very large barrels, and borrowed a knife.

"The local Italian men were amazed as their luxury food was raw broad beans, and it appeared that we were living off the 'fat of the land'. As we did not finish all our food, we shared the remainder with them, much to their delight. It was an experience, walking through the back streets of Naples as it appeared, in some respects, that we'd stepped back in time: all waste was thrown out of the windows, rubbish of all sorts was in the streets, with shoeless children and dogs running around without any cares. This was in complete contrast to the main shopping area, where modern shops were lit up with expensive clothes on show, usually next to very expensive restaurants, where their clients would be dining in evening dress, and eating and drinking the most expensive food and wine.

"The next day, the Italian Navy laid on a ferry to Capri for us. So, once again, six or eight of us took advantage of the free trip and spent the day on the island. Once ashore, we clubbed together and hired a car, with a driver, who took us round the island, dropped us off at a beach near Gracie Fields' house, and agreed to return in the afternoon. It was very pleasant lying there, occasionally sipping a glass of the local wine and observing the behaviour of the locals. One girl did attract our attention as she appeared to have more material in her hat than in her bikini!

"Eventually, our driver appeared, to pick us up. One big mistake was that he was persuaded to take a drink of our wine, and while steering the car down a mountain road with his music on, he decided to clap along to the tune, taking both hands off the wheel! Fortunately, he realised the peril we were in and so resumed steering the car in a proper manner.

"As the summer was progressing, our time left in the Mediterranean was coming to an end. Three weeks before we were due to leave, the Commander in Chief, Lord Mountbatten, came on board to say good-bye. He also wanted to interview anyone on board who had been away from England for over two years. As I had been abroad for two and a half years, I was nearly top of the list. The interview was not what I had expected, as he indicated that I was useless, as far as he was concerned.

"His point was that for most of my time in the Navy, I had been training for advancement, and we were coming to a time when some of that training could be used to the benefit of the RN. However, at that time, I had less than twelve months to complete my service contract, and I would be leaving the Navy. So he had a point.

"The day dawned when we left Malta for the last time. The ship was moored at the top end of Sliema Creek, so we had to sail down the centre of the remaining destroyers, with our paying off pennant flying from the masthead. All the crews were on deck, cheering us as we passed, and further down, the WRENS were waving to us from the Flag Officer's jetty. Our final goodbye was from the half leader, who was waiting for us outside Grand Harbour and, not only cheered us, but threw potatoes!

"Three days to Gibraltar, three days alongside and then out into the Atlantic, heading north. During this time, as I had no duties, I was working with the Coxswain, making lists of names, and various other jobs. Eventually, we turned right at Ushant to sail up the Channel, arriving at Sheerness. Once tied to a buoy, all married Petty Officers went ashore, so I was the Duty Petty Officer.

"Next day, the ship was de-ammunitioned, and the following day, proceeded to Chatham dockyard where, unlike today, two dockyard workers greeted us to take our mooring wires. Then, the whole ship's company left the ship and went on leave, for various lengths of time. I think mine was either seven or eight weeks. Although I enjoyed my leave, I was not entirely settled. On reflection, I think the reason was that I had been away for two and a half years, used to a communal life in fairly restricted surroundings and had enjoyed a certain level of independence. This attitude of mine did concern me as, in a matter of months, I would be leaving the Navy, and living with my parents, something I had not done for some years. However, more of that later...

"Leave came to an end and I returned to Chatham Barracks and joined the Petty Officers' mess. I was delighted to see many of the Chequers' Petty Officers already in residence but equally sad when, in turn, most of them left to join their new ships. There was a short period when I was employed in carrying out 'kit musters' of sailors joining the barracks from sea-going drafts – very boring and not at all pleasant. I also had to drill 'men under punishment', which meant spending an hour in the Drill Shed in the first 'dog watch', watching them doubling around the shed with a rifle. They kept warm but, as I wasn't moving, I got quite cold! I then had an interview with the drafting commander, who made various suggestions as to where I would go, but in the end, I finished up by being one of four Petty Officers in charge of the Barrack Canteen.

"It was a fairly reasonable existence. To add some spice, I was also recruited into a land fighting force. I could never really understand the reasoning of this move. To take sailors from their seagoing environment, dress them in light blue shirts and dark blue trousers, and send them to hide in an ambush in the lovely green fields seemed a bit stupid to me, especially when any foreign army invading would be crack troops! I took part in one exercise where my platoon was officially wounded. I suggested to my boys that we should retire to the local pub to 'recuperate', only to be told half an hour later that we were only wounded for ten minutes!

"Easter came and went, and normal routine continued until June/July when I was discharged from the Royal Navy. I remember having very mixed feelings. One part of me wanted to leave, but the other part was thinking, *Am I being stupid, leaving a secure job and heading into the unknown?*

"The summer of 1955 was very hot and, in Tintagel, there was a severe water shortage. For some time, we were existing on the good offices of a local farmer who delivered a churn of water to us daily until the local water board erected a tank in the field behind the house to keep us supplied. During that period and up until Christmas, I spent a lot of time repairing the banks in the field and getting the land ready to produce crops the following year. The New Year was celebrated, 1956, and the next few months were spent trying to make a living by growing 'cash crops': potatoes, salads, soft fruit, etc.

"It was around this time, early in the year, that Lilian wrote to me, saying that she had returned from Norway and was now in Plymouth. This was a very pleasant surprise, as we had not seen each other for over three years, both of us spending a lot of time abroad.

"Arrangements were made and Lilian, very bravely, came to Tintagel and spent the weekend with us. We spent most of the time walking on the cliffs, despite it being the winter. At the same time, she was studying for her Petty Officer's exam and, for a period of many weeks, was out of communication. However, the time came when she sat the exam and passed, top of the country. Fantastic!

"In the meantime, I had carried on doing all the mundane things that were required. My highlight was passing the driving test, which meant I could pick Lilian up from the station, without Father! We spent some very happy weekends together. Lilian must have liked coming to Tintagel, especially one miserable Saturday evening in the spring, when my last job before going out was to shut the ducks up in their house.

"Sods' law, of course, I had fifty ducks going in fifty different directions. It took ages to round them up and put them to bed. Meanwhile, poor Lilian was sitting in the lounge, waiting to go out. To end the story, Father had to go out in the rain to house the ones that I had missed and which were quacking like mad to go to bed!

"Lilian was promoted to WREN Petty Officer and drafted to HMS Ceres in Wetherby, Yorkshire, as an Instructor to the new entry WREN Shorthand Writers. So, we were back to telephone calls once a week. However, we did agree to meet and spend some of her Christmas leave in London, and celebrate the New Year, together. When the day came, I caught the train from Camelford to Waterloo and, to my delight, Lilian was waiting under the main clock in the station.

"We spent a very happy three or four days together – the longest time we had ever had alone! The first evening, we went to the cinema and saw the film *Battle of the River Plate*. The next day, New Year's Eve, was spent in a nightclub in Leicester Square. I had to hire a dinner suit for the occasion. Lilian was well prepared with her dress, although she spent some time looking for a new pair of shoes. Another day, we walked around Covent Garden which, in the short term, gave me a lot to think about and, ultimately, helped me to make a decision regarding my future.

"The next day, being Sunday, we caught the train to Sandwich so that Lilian could introduce me to her parents. We spent the whole day there, returning to London in the evening. The following day was our last day together. Lilian's leave was finished, and she had to return to Yorkshire on a train at midday. The only positive thought was that we had agreed to spend Easter together, wherever I was!

"On my return journey to Cornwall, the train was extremely crowded, no seats available, but a very kind ticket collector told me to sit in a first class compartment. In the fullness of time, I told my father of our visit to Covent Garden and that I had decided the time had come for me to find something else to do as I could see no future in growing plants and vegetables as I had been doing.

"A few days later, I went to the Camelford Labour Exchange and applied for a traineeship as a retail buyer in Bon Marche, Gloucester. In due course, I presented myself with my naval records to the personnel department and, after an interview, was offered a job. We agreed the date when I should start, all confirmed in writing, so I was able to return to Cornwall in a much more cheerful mood than in the past.

"In due course, the day came for me to leave Tintagel. It was a Sunday, blowing a gale and pouring with rain. I remember I got the day's supply of wood in, fed the poultry, had breakfast, finished packing and said goodbye to a dream that I had had but that had proved impossible to attain.

"I stayed in a hotel overnight and presented myself the next day to the store. There followed a day of instruction: use of tills, the company policy, and what was expected from us. I was let out early to look for somewhere to sleep. I was fortunate to find a room in Argyll Place with a Mrs. Shackleton. The room was self-contained, overlooking their back garden. All the residents ate together in the dining room, and I quickly realised that her food was something special. I learned later that her husband was a chef in a local hotel, so we dined extremely well.

"The next day, I started working in the soft furnishing department. At first, I was standing and watching how the rest of the staff behaved, but as they got busier, I had to start serving, measuring and cutting the material. After a while, it became second nature to me, and I was ready to tackle the next obstacle: changing, at regular intervals, all the displays in the department and getting the fabrics ready for display in the windows. I also had to go back to school again to study for the City and Guilds in retailing, maths, English and commodities. My final job of the day was to sweep out the stockroom and then, when the last customer had departed, I was free to go!

"A few weeks after I had started at Gloucester, we were looking forward to Easter. Before the holiday, I went with a friend, Laurie, to his home in Trowbridge to collect his car, a small pre-War Austin. We spent most of the Sunday morning trying to get it to start, pushing it down a slope and letting the clutch in.

"After some considerable time, it suddenly started and, as I did not want it to stop again, I drove off down the road for some way. To return, I obviously had to turn the car around in a three-point turn and, at the critical moment, the engine stalled. As I was trying to push the car by myself, a very kind gentleman on a bike, with two bottles of beer in his jacket pocket, offered his help. Between us, we got the car moving and, when we had built up some speed, I leapt in, put it into gear, let the clutch out and it started.

"Unfortunately, my kind rescuer had fallen over and broken one of his bottles, which stained his Sunday suit! Despite the many problems we had experienced, the car behaved itself and I was able to drive it back to Gloucester. Laurie assured me that I could borrow it over the Easter weekend and the following week, if required.

"On Maundy Thursday, Lilian arrived to stay in the Fleece Hotel for a week, so we arranged to go to Weston-super-Mare on Good Friday and have the use of the car over the weekend.

"Saturday was a working day for me but we were able to go out together for the rest of the weekend and, of course, on Easter Monday. The highlight and most important period was on the Saturday evening when, having had our evening meal, we drove to the top of Birdlip Hill, overlooking the Severn Valley and Gloucester, and parked. I proposed and Lilian said 'yes'.

"We then spent some time discussing our future and agreed to get married on Saturday October 26th 1957, and to honeymoon in Jersey. We finished the Easter break by visiting various places in the Cotswolds and then, Lilian had to return to Yorkshire. Apart from a weekend in Leicester, we did not see each other until October.

"In the meantime, I told my parents of our plans and also wrote to Lilian's parents, asking for their permission to marry their daughter.

"The big day came. At the appropriate time, my best man and I left the hotel and walked up to St Clement's Church, sat down, and waited – and waited. Lilian's car was held up at a level crossing. However, we knew all was well when the organ started to play the correct wedding music and my most beautiful bride walked up the very long centre aisle. I joined her at the altar steps. The vicar was very kind and guided us through the service, and in a very short time, we were husband and wife. After photographs and the reception, we caught the train to London, where we stayed in the same hotel as we had done earlier in the year. This time, however, in a double room.

"We spent our honeymoon in the Fort d'Auvergne Hotel in Jersey, just outside St Helier and enjoyed a lovely time. We toured the whole island in a hired car, suffering a puncture in Gorey, and, although it was late October, were able to sit and relax on the cliffs, overlooking Corbière Lighthouse. Our time in Jersey was coming to an end and we had to come back down to earth.

"Our first night in the flat was a bit of an anti-climax. We had been promised two wool blankets as a wedding present and were assured they would be waiting for us on our return. Needless to say, they were not. In fact, we are still waiting for them! We spent our first night in Gloucester, cuddling under my ten year old naval blanket and two overcoats.

"My career moved on apace and I was interviewed for a job as a Soft Furnishing Buyer in the Debenhams store, Spooners, in Plymouth. Mother and Father joined me for the evening at the Grand Hotel, and we had dinner. During breakfast the next morning, I was able to watch a flotilla of destroyers sailing out of the harbour. Happy days! On my return to Gloucester, Lilian was able to confirm that her doctor had said that she was pregnant.

"Our lives were changed when Janice was born on Saturday May 28th, 1960, in the Alexandra Maternity Home. Although she was born fairly early in the morning, I did not know until nearly midday when a nurse from the home phoned me at work.

"Janice was the first girl to be born in my family since 1903, and my parents, especially Mother, were thrilled to have a granddaughter. Of course, Lilian and I were unable to go out together very much, as we did not know enough people to ask someone to babysit. However, a very kind lady who lived opposite realised our problems and she very kindly offered to look after Janice when we wanted to go out. She became known as Auntie Palmer and she became a very good friend to us.

"Time passed, and I was finding my position at work very difficult. Despite my best efforts, I was not achieving my targets, which was causing a certain amount of friction between the MD and me, which I was very worried about. The crunch came in the following March when all the store buyers were interviewed by the MD to discuss their figures and to be given their commission cheques. My interview did not go well and I finished up by agreeing I should leave as my position had become untenable. To my surprise, I still received a commission cheque well into three figures. After a few weeks and writing various letters, I was offered a job as a representative for a company called Hanson Sales Ltd, my area being the South West and South Wales.

"The following Monday, I caught an early train to London to join Hanson sales. I spent four days there and returned to Plymouth, driving a new-ish Ford. As it was a fine weekend, Lilian agreed we should spend some time on the beach, so we piled into the car, making sure we not only had food, but all the bits and pieces Janice would require.

"It was a happy time for us. For the first time since we had been married, I had the whole weekend off and we could do as we liked. Monday came and my first call was to be in Taunton where I opened my first account. Also, of course, I had my first sale. Fantastic. I stayed with Hanson Sales for just over two years.

"Andrew was born, to our great delight in the November of 1962. It was a very hard winter, which started on Boxing Day with a blizzard, and continued with snowfall and hard frosts until the end of February. It was just after this that we heard of a house to let and, in due course, we signed the lease and moved in at the beginning of April.

"Just after we moved to this village, in 1963, I was asked by a neighbour, Colonel Clayton, if I had served in the Forces. On learning that I had, he enrolled me into the local Legion Branch.

"I did not attend any meetings, due to work commitments, but Lilian persuaded me to attend an AGM the following year and, to my great surprise, I was elected Branch Vice Chairman, proposed by a founder member and First World War veteran.

"During the next couple of years, I became more interested in the Legion, attending Group meetings and visiting other Branches. In the fullness of time, I was elected Chairman and began to attend the County Conferences, during which, I got to know the County Officers. Time passed, and in 1971, we received an invitation to a Buckingham Palace Garden Party to celebrate the first fifty years of the organisation. We were both very surprised and delighted and, of course, accepted.

"On the day, which was very hot, we drove to London with two friends, stopped at a hotel to change, had lunch, then continued in to the City, where I was able to park the car opposite the Palace. We then had a group photo taken and lined up in a queue to enter the Palace gardens. A high point of the afternoon was when the Queen, as she was leaving the garden, stood on the veranda and announced that the British Legion would, in future, be known as the Royal British Legion. All members present were delighted and cheered the announcement.

"Moving on, I progressed through the ranks by becoming a member of the County Committee, and also Otter Group Chairman. After three years, I put myself forward for election as a County Officer and was elected three years later. In the meantime, I was still very active in the Branch and was presented with a Legion Gold Badge, by the County Chairman, at a Poppy evening. I was also delighted that Andrew, our son, who had taken part in fifteen-mile sponsored walks was awarded a special silver cup to thank him and mark his achievements in raising so much money for the Poppy Appeal.

"At about this time, I resigned as Branch Chairman after an upset with the Secretary, who also stood down. The result of the major change was that I became Branch Secretary, a position I held for twelve years. I was delighted that in my time as Secretary, the Branch won the Group, County, South West Area and National Efficiency cups, not once, but several times.

"I also organised sponsored walks for the Poppy Appeal, as well as many other events, including the Branch Annual Flower Show and Fete. In the meantime, I was advancing up towards being the County Chairman. Out of the ordinary jobs, apart from attending sports events, fetes, dinners and Branch meetings all over the County, I was chairing appeals by members who had misbehaved in some way, often through drink. I found it very interesting and enlightening.

"Time moved on, and becoming County Chairman meant that I also served on the South West Area Council, which entailed travelling over the five counties (Devon, Cornwall, Somerset, Wiltshire and Dorset) to attend appeals and other activities.

"It was about this time that I was awarded a National Life Member's badge and certificate. My climb upwards was confirmed when I was elected South West Area Vice Chairman and then, two years later, became Chairman.

"My election to the Chairman's position coincided with the seventieth anniversary of the Legion, and Lilian and I were invited to all the five counties celebrations, and also a thanksgiving service in Westminster Abbey, sitting in reserved seats. We also attended our third Buckingham Palace Garden Party!

"During my term of Area Office, HQ announced the closing of the Area structure. They also appointed a new position of County Field Officer, to look after the welfare cases. The last Area Conference that I chaired was very bad-tempered and hostile, mainly because of the demise of the area organisation and the uncertainty of the future.

"However, I wasn't quite finished as Lilian and I attended the National Conference, where I chaired a national appeal and was also presented with a National Certificate of Merit, the Legion's highest award. We were also invited to attend another Palace Garden Party.

"At about this time, I was coming up to retirement, 1995. My boss, Cornelia James was very kind and, apart from inviting Lilian and me to lunch at her house, she also presented me with a cut-glass bowl at a staff get-together the next day. The pub in Pevensey, that I had stayed in many times during the period I had been employed by Cornelia James, let us stay there free of charge and also gave us their best room, with a four-poster bed.

"We returned home just in time to go to Northern Cyprus for a fortnight, while an extension was being built onto the end of the house. It was great to get away in the sun and to return to Kyrena for the first time since 1949. We hired a car and explored most of the area. We also spent many hours on the beach. Bliss! Incidentally, we returned to Northern Cyprus many times during the following years and enjoyed it just as much.

"On our return home, we were faced with cleaning up after all the building works, as well as painting the outside and interior walls. We settled into a way of life once we were both home and retired. I became more involved with outside activities, such as the RBL County Festival of Remembrance, and the County War Pensions Committee.

"I was also involved in the County Golf Tournament as Treasurer. This was held at the Woodbury Golf Club, owned by Nigel Mansell, the Formula One racing driver, on Woodbury Common. The first tournament was held during the following year and was very successful but after that, we struggled and it was eventually disbanded.

"Life continued quietly until November, when I learnt that the Poppy Appeal Organiser in Exeter had resigned about a fortnight before the big day. Panic! However, Tim Courtenay organised some volunteers and David Walker and I spent at least three days delivering Poppy Boxes to the various shops and other outlets in the City Centre. I also spent some hours in the city with a box of poppies, standing outside the local Boots shop on the High Street. Happy days!

"Following this period, time flew and Lilian and I were very happy on the arrival of our eldest granddaughter, Lara. Twelve months later, our second granddaughter, Briony, was born – again, to our delight. We were able to spend time with both of them. To complete the family, two years later, Jeremy was born. All our grandchildren are doing very well in their chosen careers and seem to be destined for bright futures.

"Time passed, we went on holiday to Northern Cyprus at varying times of the year, and continued in various capacities, supporting the Legion at County level. It was during this period that I received a letter from the Prime Minister's Office, informing me that I had been awarded the MBE for services to the Royal British Legion in Devon. Needless to say, I was highly delighted by the news and also, I was the first Legion member in Devon to be honoured with such an award.

"Six weeks later, when the honours were published, I was inundated with phone calls and letters from the great and the good within Devon, and the Legion's National President. Lilian decided that, as if was a one off, we should celebrate in style. So, we arranged with Janice and Andrew to stay in London the night before the investiture and, on the day, to take lunch at the Savoy. The hotel supplied a stretched limo to pick us up, so we arrived in style.

"The investiture was not so nerve-racking as one imagined. I knew that Lilian and the family had obtained front seats in the Throne Room, while I was in a beautifully decorated anteroom being instructed by an Equerry on the correct way to answer the Prince of Wales, and the way to bow. After that, it was a matter of waiting, watching the investiture taking place in the Throne Room on the internal TVs, and chatting to the other recipients.

"In the end, it turned out that I was nearly last in the last group to be called. Having lined up, we walked in a roundabout route to the Throne Room and then, waited for our names to be called. After an interval, my name was called and, after the requisite bow, the Prince attached the award to my jacket and surprised me by talking about the Royal Navy! We spoke about various events, a final shake of hands, three steps back, bow, turn right and walk out, passing Lilian and family, sitting in the front row. I met up with them a few minutes later, and we all posed for photographs in front of the Palace before travelling back to the Savoy.

"We gathered in the bar and ordered drinks. I am not certain what I expected but I was surprised by the prices. Andrew's half-pint of beer was over two pounds fifty! However, we had lunch, which we all enjoyed and, as it was a special occasion, we had two bottles of wine (house).

"A very memorable event finished the lunch when the waiter presented us with a dish of chocolate balls, filled with ice cream. I explained that I had not ordered them, but he assured me that they were 'on the house' in honour of the occasion. That small gesture rounded off a very memorable day and I was very touched by his thoughtfulness and kindness.

"We left the Savoy by taxi, returning to our hotel to get changed and say goodbye to Andrew, who was returning home to Worcester. Before he left, he gave us a set of photograph frames to keep a record of the day.

"We went by taxi from the hotel to Waterloo Station and Lilian explained to the driver why we were in London. As a parting present, he only charged us ten pounds. At least thirteen pounds was showing on the meter."

Ray

"AS A VERY YOUNG LAD, I lived in Dartmouth. In those days, the Dartmouth Squadron were about, and there were about five ships. We lived quite high up, overlooking the river. I don't know whether you know Dartmouth at all, but as you come in from the castle it goes around a corner where the ferries meet at what we used to call The Bite. Well, as the ships came round this bend in the river, they used to let out the *whoop-whoop-whoop* which, to me, was a fascinating thing. I used to hear the sound and rush straight up into my mother's bedroom, which was at the front of the house, and I'd watch these ships coming in. I suppose, in a way, that led me towards a naval life.

"Because I can't really say that my father influenced me, although he was in the Navy. I think it was at my parents' silver wedding, as the eldest child, I had to give a speech. And so, when I gave the speech, I said I thought we ought to thank our mother for bringing us up because, for three-quarters of our lives, our father wasn't there.

"Anyway, I got to the age of about fifteen and my father asked me what I was going to do with my life. We could leave school at sixteen, and most people did. I think you had to have four GCEs to go to the sixth form. This was at grammar school, of course. I was coming up to that age, and he asked me what I might do and I said I thought I might join the Navy.

"*'As what?'* he asked.

"*'Same as you,'* I said. *'A sailor.'*

"*'Don't be so stupid.'*

"So, I said, *I've thought about joining the Fleet Air Arm, as a pilot.*'

"He said, *That's even worse.*'

"I thought it sounded wonderful – to be up, over the waves, with that sense of freedom but he said he'd known of too many young lads who'd been killed.

"I said, *Well, when your number's up, your number's up.*'

"He said, *There's no point in hurrying it.*'

"So he asked me if I wanted to join as an artificer. I didn't know what an artificer was. He explained that it would mean joining up as a trades-man and learning a trade. He actually sent away for the booklet and, when it arrived, I flipped through it and read about engineers, electricians, radar and then I saw these blokes making canoes and I thought, *That'll do me.*'

"You could take the entrance exam before the GCEs. The entrance exam was supposed to be the equivalent of maths, science and English. Well, I was all right at maths, but I was only doing general science at school, without much enthusiasm. I was learning general science from the headmaster who was a dickhead and didn't like me very much, so I thought I'd need to learn more on the mechanical side of science.

"So, I went to see the physics teacher, told him what I was planning to do and asked if I could borrow a physics textbook. It was a great book, which covered elementary mechanics and I read it right the way through. At the end of each chapter, there was a Question and Answer section, and I did those. Didn't cheat. It was like a *Teach Yourself...* set-up.

"Two of us went for the entrance exam and we both passed. Then, we had to go to Portsmouth, for four days, to do an aptitude test. So, this headmaster, who didn't like me, was quite keen that we defer our entry to the Navy, in order that we could come back to school and take our GCEs beforehand.

"This other lad and I went to Portsmouth. The other lad was the blue-eyed boy. He could do nothing wrong. Believe it or not, he failed the aptitude test. I passed – well, it was all to do with mechanics and I'd been reading up.

"If you imagine, you're in groups of about twenty-five and the first thing that happened, they sat us down and told us, *'Out of you twenty-five, we'll probably take four.'*

"I was interviewed by a woman at one stage and she said, *'I see you go to Churston Grammar School and... oh, I see your father's in the Navy and... your sister's nursing...'* And as a young boy of sixteen, I had no idea how they could know all this. I was absolutely amazed, she was just turning page after page and telling me about my life. Talk about Big Brother – and in those days!

"We came towards the end of the tests. Some of it was common sense. My name was the first one called out and I was led to a room, sat down, and they asked if I'd ever been in trouble with the police. I hadn't. I was told I'd been accepted, but they wanted to ask if I would like to defer my entry for the GCEs. No chance. I wasn't going back to school.

"So my entry date was set at 6th May. I came home, obviously chuffed to bits. The other lad went back to school, of course. When the head-master called the register at school, he got to my name and the other lad told him I'd left to join the Navy.

"I then had three years of school. I had a year at Fisgard in Cornwall. I mean, that's a story. Coming from a Naval family, I was brought up with discipline, no slacking off.

"There were three classes, each four months long. So the top class, who'd been there for all of eight months, decided there would be an initiation for us sprogs – who'd only just arrived.

"Inside each block, it was a big, long dormitory, and there was a blast wall. There were open beams, so you could see right the way through – the whole length of the room. And these guys, in their wisdom, had sharpened the first beam. The idea was, you'd climb up onto the blast wall, jump and catch the beam.

"So the first bloke went up, jumped, caught the beam and – cut both his hands. And then, one of them turned round to me, because I was next in line for the initiation.

"Well, there was no way. And I told him so, very succinctly.

"He said, *'Who do you think you're talking to?'*

"*'Some idiot,'* I said. *'If you think I'm going to go up there, jump off and get hurt, just so you can have a laugh, you've got another think coming.'*

"*'But you've got to,'* the idiot said. *'We're in three class, and you're only in one class.'*

"So, I pointed out how many of us there were, because ours was a big entry, and certainly, compared to the number of them, we massively outnumbered them. And I asked the rest of the blokes in my class if they wanted to do it.

"From that point on, my nickname was Strop, because I was a stroppy git, and it stuck with me until I went into the Fleet.

"With the training, Fisgard was one side of the road. On the other side of the road was HMS Raleigh. At that time, my father was the Gunnery Officer of HMS Raleigh. The only reason we had to go to HMS

Raleigh was the post office. If we wanted any money, we didn't go to the bank, we went to the post office.

"They had two brass canons, which is where the Officer of the Day was. Even if the Officer of the Day wasn't stood there, in the Navy, we have this tradition of saluting the quarterdeck on the ship. So this area with the brass canons was, in effect, the quarterdeck. So, as we marched in – we didn't stroll – as we *marched* in, we stopped and saluted the quarterdeck.

"A friend and I went several times. He was a Scotsman, an artificer, and this one day, we marched over, saluted the quarterdeck, and this voice said, '*Halt!*'

"I recognised it as my father's voice.

"'*Where are you two lads going?*'

"'*To the post office, sir.*'

"'*Why?*'

"'*To get some money, sir.*'

"'*Why?*'

"There was a pause. '*Well, it's my money, sir.*'

"'*Carry on.*'

"Now, when I passed out, to go to the Caledonia, I was six foot tall and I was always in the guard. You fall in three deep, and then you form twos. I was always in the front rank and we'd file out, get into two ranks, so I wound up as the third one from the end. We were just getting ready to go on parade with all the gear on, and this Chief GI came along – he was about your size."

<Me: I'm five foot four.>

"And he said, *'The Gunnery Officer of HMS Raleigh is going to inspect the guard.'*

"So, I thought, *'Do we really need this?'* But we were stood to attention, very smart, and my father did his inspection. The top of his hat came up to almost my eyebrows.

"He said, *'Your boots aren't very clean, lad.'*

"I said, *'I don't think they're that bad, sir.'*

"*'Not as good as mine,'* he said.

"*'But I did mine myself, sir.'* Strop, you see. This Chief GI nearly pissed himself.

"Anyway, my father carried on and marched to the parade ground, with his sword and everything. And he saw Barbara, sitting in the front row. So he saluted, everyone was looking, and he sat down next to her and gave her a kiss.

"So then, I passed out and was off to HMS Caledonia, where it starts all over again. The people who had been in our three class were still two classes above us. They were the top dogs when we got there because they'd won various trophies every term... until we arrived. And then, it was our turn.

"The school was one of the top training establishments, and there were factories down the bottom of the hill. We used to fall in outside the factories and then march up the hill. I'm sure it wasn't just me but, in fact, we were known as the stroppiest division there was.

"So word would come from the Chief Stoker, *'Permission to carry on. First division, stand fast.'* And so we'd wait, expecting a bollocking for too much chatter or whatever it was, while they all marched off. And then he'd say, *'First division, right turn, double, march!'* and we'd go up and down this hill, for about half-hour at a time. This meant that we were probably the fittest division in the establishment, which is probably why we started winning all the cups and trophies.

"I had started playing hockey. Our Divisional Chief came in and he said that we were short for the rugby team that day, did anyone want to play? So, I said that I'd played rugby at school, and with that, I was in the rugby team. I ended up playing for about six terms.

"I wound up having several operations on my back. After the fifth of these, I had to go to Edinburgh for my review, and an Army Captain asked if I'd had any discharge from the wound.

"*'Well,'* I said, *'only yesterday, when I played rugby.'*

"Once I'd scraped him off the ceiling, it was a case of – *'You will never, ever play rugby again.'* So that was the end of my rugby days, although it was often very tempting to go back. Fortunately, I could swim.

"In those days, if the weather was inclement, nine times out of ten, we'd have to go on a run. I used to hate cross-country running and I think it's the only thing in my life that I've ever cheated on. We used to cheat every time because it was so dull. However, occasionally, we would have a swimming gala. Now, because we were good swimmers, the boss would ask me to pick twenty blokes to swim.

"I said to him, *'How come, when we have cross-country, everybody's got to do it, but when it's a swimming gala, there'll only be twenty men?'* Because it made no sense. Everybody could swim. Of course we could.

"Anyway, I did all the lifesaving medals and won awards and that sort of thing. There was a challenge where we had to do thirty lengths in – I think it was half an hour. Well, I did it in thirteen minutes. I was always a good swimmer.

"Then, I went into the Fleet. The first ship I had was HMS Victorious, in Portsmouth. She'd just come in. She'd been out of commission and had had a refit. We were in Portsmouth Docks. I was going up and down, every weekend. We slept on board HMS Centaur, which was an old aircraft carrier, and she was that old, and that infested with cockroaches, that any time you took anything out of your locker, you'd have to shake it to make sure the cockroaches were out of it. You'd have to sweep them out of your bed. Anyway, having persevered through all of that, I moved into the ventilation.

"One of my first jobs was as a chimney sweep, and I started in the laundry. It was a bit like getting into a tumble dryer, full of fluff, and I could see a little hole at the top. So, my job was to de-fluff the thing and progress through the ventilation shaft. Now, this laundry was on five deck – so called because it was five decks down – and the outlet came out underneath the flight deck. I had to crawl through this trunking, with a mask on, sweeping behind me just like an old-fashioned chimney sweep and, eventually, I could see daylight. So, I got to the end and then I had to stop, and move on to the next one. By the time I'd finished, I knew every ventilation system, inside and out, and from any point in the trunking, I could tell you exactly where I was on the ship.

"Barbara and I had got married by this point. The reason we got married then was because you got more money when you were away – because, originally, we were going to get married when I came back – but I was going to be away for eighteen months or so.

"A week before the Commissioning Service, I was home, turned on the radio in the morning and heard the headline – *Fire On HMS Victorious Still Not Under Control.*

"What had happened was, the fire had started underneath the flight deck. They reckoned that a tea urn had boiled dry and the solder had come out of the bottom and caused this fire. Unfortunately, in those days, there was only one door to the mess. One man was killed. He collapsed with the smoke, fell in the water and he was boiled to death.

"After that, it was determined that every door in the Navy had to be fitted with an escape panel and there had to be two exits to every space. Because that was probably what had happened to this chap. He would have gone to the furthest corner, away from the blaze, and been trapped.

"This fire had burned a good third of the way through the ship. If you imagine the flight deck, it was about an inch and a half thick, to take the weight of the aircraft. If you looked at it after the fire, it was like a piece of corrugated iron. After the fire, they scrapped it. So, our Commissioning Day was the farewell. We never went to sea on her, which was a shame because, having spent two years working on it – it was a beautiful ship, it really was. It's funny, you know, these silly sailors getting attached to their ships.

"I was very briefly on the Hermes, as many others were. Unfortunately, my back problem returned, so I ended up in Haslar Hospital in Portsmouth. So, I never went away on her.

"Then, we went back to Devonport. After cleaning out all this laundry stuff on Victorious, they put me to work in the laundry on Drake. There was a lot of teaching there: teaching sailors how to operate the machines, which was good because we needed things to wash, for training. So, on the lunchtime, I would go down into the dockyards and see all my mates from different ships, stop and have a beer, pick up their washing, take it back and bring it back for them the next day, cleaned, pressed, everything. Didn't cost them anything. Maybe a couple of beers.

"And then I was due to go to the Far East. I was a Petty Officer then, and I was told I had to go and do a leadership course in the Brecon Beacons. So, I asked why. It didn't seem necessary, given that I'd been a Petty Officer for eight months. Plus, I'd just got a draft to the Far East. It was going to be quite physical, this leadership course, and I'd had five or six operations on my back. Of course, I didn't want to go up there and end up in hospital. So, I was sent to see the doctor. He was having none of it. Told me I couldn't risk taking the course and damaging my back again. So, I passed my leadership course without going on it.

"I ended up going to Singapore. I was on HMS Forth, which was built in 1939, so it was older than me. She was a lovely old ship, a Submarine Depot Ship. We could actually, if we'd wanted to, build a submarine on board the ship. We had all the presses and foundries because that was the job, during the War. Of course, she'd survived the War and was a grand old lady of the sea, and we had some good times on board.

"We'd only been there a few weeks. Barbara was there, six months pregnant when we went to Bangkok. And in a couple of months, I'd been to Malaya, Thailand... I'd been away for a while and came back. Making love, as you do, and she said, *'It's coming.'*

"I said, *'I know.'*

"She said, *'Not you. The baby!'*

"So, there was a mad panic because I didn't have a car in those days. I had to run through the jungle to wake my mate, whose wife was already in the hospital, to get him to take us there in his car. It was very sad because he and his wife had lost their baby the day before my son was born. That's why she is godmother to our first child.

"And, of course, the next thing was we went to Hong Kong. First of all, my boss asked if my father was at the gunnery range. So, I said yes. He replied that he'd just wondered. And when I got back, there was a letter from my dear mother, saying, *'Would you believe it? We're coming out there. Your father's got an appointment – to HMS Forth.'*

"We knew we were going to Australia. And my dad was a bit like me – it was always: *been there, ticked it off.* But we were going to Australia and I knew my father had never been there. So, I was finally going somewhere he'd never been. And what happened? He joined the Forth and we went and saw it together.

"The funny thing was, when we got back on board the next day, I turned to my boss and said, *'You knew he was joining, didn't you?'*

"He said, *'Well, I couldn't say anything. If you want to leave, you can try something else, I can fix it for you.'*

"I said, *'I was on this ship first.'* It was my ship before it was his ship. Anyway, it was quite amusing at times because whenever we wanted an extra drink, we'd call my father. Because we were only allowed two pints at sea, but if we called him down, he'd come along and offer everyone else a drink, so we'd all get an extra one.

"We went up to Bangkok, to a place at the mouth of the river. We drew about eighteen foot, and since the river going up to Bangkok was quite shallow, we had to offload fuel to get her higher in the water. We went to an American Army base there, but our leave expired at midnight.

"As we were coming back to the ship, we realised we were late. By the time we got back, we weren't allowed on board. Now, unbeknownst to us, the Duty Commanding Officer was dear Dad. His Officer of the Day was drunk, so he had to deal with him and he wasn't in the best of moods. When we arrived, we were only actually five minutes late, and we had to fall in, three deep, on the quarterdeck. By this time, my nickname had changed from Strop to Ted, and one of my mates told me that I'd be all right because it was my dad who was in charge. In fact, it was probably worse.

"So, my father told the assembly that it wasn't good enough, that as Petty Officers, we should know better than coming in late, all this – and then he saw me. And that was it – boom – our eyes locked. And he went on and on and on, and then he turned to his NCI – a Naval policeman, if you like – and said, *'Get them off my quarterdeck, now!'*

"The next day, there had to be a report made to the Captain, and this sneaky little Naval copper gave the report. He said, *'There were forty Petty Officers late back, sir, including the Gunnery Officer's son.'* So, the Captain spoke to my father.

"*'Everything all right last night?'* the Captain asked.

"And my father told him everything had been fine.

"*'I thought there were some Petty Officers who came aboard late?'*

"He said, *'I don't know who's told you that, sir. As you know, I was the Duty Commanding Officer of this ship last night and, as far as I'm concerned, there were no Petty Officers out late.'*

"*'Very good,'* said the Captain. *'Carry on.'*

"At this point, I was in the mess and the phone went. It was Dad and he said he thought I should invite him down for a drink at lunchtime. It was the policeman's mess, but he wasn't there. When we finally found him, my father said to the policeman, *'I want a word with you.'*

"*'What's that, sir?'* the policeman said, all innocence, you know.

"And I have never seen a man pulled apart like that. The way my father went after this policeman, in front of his mates, this bloke must have felt about an inch big. By the end of this speech, my father said, *'You never do that kind of thing, going behind the Commanding Officer's back to the Captain. Everyone else is welcome to a drink, but you're not having one.'* And that was that.

"We were coming home together, a steaming crew, and we went into a little island, a coral atoll called Diego Garcia. We went in first thing in the morning, it was beautiful, and our job when we got in was to lower the ladders from the quarterdeck. My dad was the quarterdeck officer. So, we were just ambling in and I was looking over the side – the water was so clear, you could see the sea bed and all the fish. Stunning. And my dad came alongside me and said, '*It hasn't changed much since '47.*'

"He'd been there as well! We'd never even heard of this place, and he'd been! There was nowhere, really, that we could go to that he hadn't already seen. But the last time he'd been there, leaning over the side to look at this clear water, I was at home, being born.

"After this stop-off in Diego Garcia, I was home for six months before joining the Lynx. We brought the Lynx in because she needed repairs because she was leaking. She had these two big stabilisers that came out, about as big as the bar here – if it was rough, these stabilisers would come out. Anyway, she'd developed a leak and it was our job to fix her.

"What we decided to do was get some half-inch plate and roll it into the shape of the ship's hull. Then, we cut up some mattresses and put them all the way round the inside, to act like insulation, and then we took this half-inch plate and lowered it with cables, and we winched it into place and brought her home. And six months later, my draft came through and I'd got the Lynx. Well, I knew that ship very well. She was classed as a slum ship because there was never a bunk for every man on board. There were six of us in my mess, and we could just about fit two more bunks in there. The Chippy used to sleep in the workshop. There was no air conditioning so we used to put a windscoop out (a windscoop is a scoop-shaped device that is clipped on to the air port of a ship to bring direct outside air into the ship) and, as the wind came up, it would cool the bunk. Sometimes, if the sea got rough, the water would come in and we'd wake up to wet beds.

"I remember getting back to this country. We went up to Worthington and just down from where we were berthed, there was a Labour Club. It was when Harold Wilson's lot were in charge. A couple of our blokes had gone into this Club and met an MP, who just happened to be the Minister for Agriculture and Fisheries. These blokes invited him to come back to the ship the next day. He was invited for a drink in the Stokers' mess and the Captain was there, and this Minister asked where we all slept.

"We all pointed. *'Well, you're sitting on his bed, and your drink is on so-and-so's bed, that's another bed over there,'* and so forth.

"He was surprised. *'But what does your union say about this?'* he asked.

"And we looked at each other. Of course, we didn't have a union and we told him so.

"*'I'll sort that out,'* he said. Incredible.

"We went out to Greece on a NATO exercise. In those days, we should have worn uniform, but we went to shore in civvies because we weren't supposed to be there. There was a bit of trouble between the Greeks and the Turks and they were both in the exercise together. There were six of us, and the Captain called for a driver for us. Eventually, we got one, and we met these people up the coast – holidaymakers. Among them was a girl who asked us where we were staying. She thought we were like her and staying in a hotel. So, we pointed to the water and said, *'Do you see that ship?'*

"*'What, that big grey one?'* she asked. And then, the penny dropped. She said, *'I wondered what that flag was.'*

"Anyway, we ended up singing. They kept us singing all night, we did all sea shanties and we didn't buy any beer or anything. The next night, we went back again. We walked in and the place was full. There was so much excitement and they had us sing for them again. And then the beer started. It was like International Cabaret: Stars of the Aegean.

"After all this, I was very nicely suntanned, and thinking about summer leave, back on the beaches, and we were sent to Iceland. It was a diesel ship, with the exhaust coming out from the mast. It was quite amusing because a lot of people thought we couldn't go fast because they didn't realise we were a diesel ship.

"Anyway, there was a pennant on the side of the ship – it went yellow-blue-blue-yellow – and that was a symbol of Fisheries Protection. In the top yellow section, there should have been an NE, to signify the area we were in.

"Now, the dockyard had fitted this pennant – upside down – so it was blue-yellow-yellow-blue, which meant a totally different thing. It didn't mean distress, like with a national flag, it just meant that we didn't have the authorisation to be in the area we were. Except we did. We realised this, going into Rosyth. One of the trawlers signalled to tell us. Of course, we had to change it.

"So, they winched me up in a boatswain's chair (which is basically a plank of wood, with ropes attached). I had to take the pennants off, turn them around and fix them properly. But the boat was rolling and pitching.

"We did six weeks up there and we had the reputation as the only ship that had been up there and not been hit. We also had a reputation because the Sun and the Daily Mirror had reported that we'd had an encounter. One of the gunboats had a bloke on it who was an absolute nutter, and he had opened up on one of the big trawlers. Maybe it was a tug.

"He didn't hit her, as such, but we had two big twin 45 turrets. As we got closer, the old turrets went up and the Admiralty was signalled.

And they refused permission to fire. The sailors were quite hacked off because the old adrenaline was going, so what happened was: they broke open the veg stocks and took out all the swedes, and started hurling them at this gunboat. A couple of them hit the bridge windows, which cracked. The headline was *'Navy Uses New Missiles'*.

"Our skipper was such a character, a great bloke, we'd follow him to the ends of the earth. There were other ships that used to go to Reykjavik every weekend, and we'd hold a blockade to watch them go in, so we knew where they were. Now, our skipper was sticking to the rule of the road, as it were, giving way and such, and we watched them heading in, but they hadn't signalled correctly and so we turned them back out. And we kept them out for about four hours. This was quite entertaining, because they'd start to move and we'd turn them back out. We were watching from the upper deck. He was a brilliant seaman, our skipper, because he kept turning them round. Whether they got in front or behind, wherever they went, he would move them. After four hours of it, he let them carry on.

"We had quite an experience once. The whaler went out to fix a trawler that had got into difficulties. The message came through, *'Thanks very much for your help, I'll send you some cod.'*

"Well, our skipper was fed up with cod. We had freezers full of it. We lived on cod. So the message came through, *'Is there anything else you would like?'* And the skipper signalled back that he liked halibut. *'No problem,'* came the reply, *'I'll send you some.'*

"It was the biggest fish I've ever seen. A huge flat fish and we had to use a winch to get it on board. It fed the whole ship's company: 220 men. And there was some to spare. It was beautiful.

"You see, when you're on a ship, you never notice how much you're moving. Your body just acclimatises. Going into Cape Town on the way home, and – I'd never known anything like it because, as I say, on the ship, you don't notice – but you can understand when these lone yachtsmen can't stand up when they've been on a long voyage around the world. Once we were off the ship, we looked across at Table Mountain, and it was moving. It took three days off the ship for the mountain to stop moving.

"From there, we went to St Helena and Tristan da Cunha. The thing with St Helena, we were only in there about a day, and the rabble went ashore. Of course, there's only one town on St Helena and one pub. So, we went ashore around lunchtime, the pub was open and the mayor of the island was in there. Suddenly, two o'clock, two hundred sailors turned up. We had to be back to the ship by four but the landlord of the pub told us he was closing up and half past two. Had a little chat with the mayor and he granted the pub an extension, because they came under British law back then, so his word was enough to keep the place open 'til four, or until the beer ran out, whichever came first. Of course, they ran out of beer first. They had to wait a week for their delivery ship to bring more, so they must have drunk spirits for the rest of the week because there wasn't a drop of ale left on the island. But the landlord was very happy.

"There was another trip when we went to Ascension. That was amazing because we weren't allowed ashore so we did some fishing. You've never seen so many fish. The trouble was, these fish ate – well, the ship's toilets discharged into the sea. These were what were known as triggerfish. They were flat and black, with these enormous buck teeth. But you'd pull the flush, and these fish would go mad, chasing what was discharged from the ship.

"We decided to have a fishing competition. There were so many of these triggerfish, as soon as you put something in the water, something bit it. There was one guy who ended up with the cover of a fan, which he put on some string with a bit of meat in it, and just dragged it through the water. He must have caught dozens. There were buckets and buckets of triggerfish. Aside from being unappetising – because of what they'd been eating – these fish were rock-hard. Completely inedible, but we gave them to the laundrymen, who dried them.

"We sailed at midnight. Of course, in the tropics, the portholes were open. We had lights on the bottom of the ladders and these fish would gather around the lights, the water was teaming with them. And the water was so clear, they were perfectly visible. When the blokes were going down to the workshops, because they'd left these portholes open, there were fish everywhere. Flying fish about ten inches long had flown in and covered the floor of the workshop. Well, they were all right, we could eat them.

"I went to the Gambia, briefly, and then I went back out to the Far East, around the Cape again, around South Africa. We went to Simon's Town, not Cape Town, and then spent six weeks on pirate patrol. The Rhodesians, in those days... were you alive then?"

<Me: I have no idea. What year are we up to?>

"This is in the seventies."

<Me: We're still waiting for me. I like to think I was thought of.>

"Rhodesia (as it was known back then) had declared independence, and there was a blockade of Mombasa. Because she was a slum ship, within a day of being on board, we ran out of fresh water. Of course, we had to make our own, distilling and processing. We all ended up with a basin full of water a day. No showers. It makes me laugh when people say you should drink more water because we weren't allowed. It's surprising what the body gets used to.

"It was the beauty of being on a diesel ship. We used to shut down the engines and just drift. It's not like a steam ship where you have to keep the turbines going. With a diesel ship, you'd just press the button and start her up, bit like a car in that way. So we just drifted for about six weeks and did some fishing, started the engine up and we were off.

"There was a sort of a First Lieutenant who was a bit – well, we received a mayday from some Korean fishermen who'd got stuck on an island. So, we went to get them off and rescue their trawler. We sent the ship's whaler to go and pick them up and this First Lieutenant, who was a right whatsit, took the whaler in, the wrong way, and it ended up capsizing. One of the Chiefs dived in after him, because he was all tangled up in ropes, and the Chief saved his life. The Chief was sent to Coventry by the rest of us for not letting him die. He was bloody awful.

"Another time, we had a Master-at-Arms – that was the only ship I've been on where there was actually a mutiny... He treated the ship's company as if we were all still wet behind the ears. He was going down into the Stokers' mess at six o'clock in the morning, turning on all the lights and getting them out of bed. Well, they'd been watch-keeping, and had only been to bed at 4am. So it got to the stage where the engineer had to have a word. The Master-at-Arms insisted he was only doing his job and the engineer told him, *'On your head be it.'*

"So, soon after this, he went down to the Stokers' mess in the morning, switched all the lights on, and found four-hundred sailors waiting for him. Well, he got out quickly and they pulled the hatch down and refused to come out. Of course, they had to get the engineer. He was a smashing bloke, he was like an old school-master. So, he came down and said, *'What seems to be the problem?'*

"He knew damn well what the problem was but he needed to hear it. Then, he said he'd have to get the Captain. The sailors were fine with that suggestion. Needless to say, the Captain gave the Master-at-Arms a good talking-to.

"Normally, the Master-at-Arms is like the chief of police and has a place in the ceremonies. The ship's rugby team, who were big buggers, summoned the Master-at-Arms, and he was hiding. When they found him, they dragged him along, they got him to the end of the gun deck and threw him down. He was a changed man after that.

"We went on to Singapore, this was after nearly two and a half months at sea. Of course, we used to get paid back then in cash but, in effect, we hadn't been paid because there wasn't the money on board. So, when we were going ashore, we were owed quite a lot, but they wouldn't give us more than two days' pay, because they knew some would go ashore and blow the lot.

"The other thing on that ship was where we come to the expression – *'Fifteen years of undetected crime'*. My workshop was underneath the fore turret. They used to have shooting practice and there was an escape panel – you remember, I was telling you about the escape panels that were introduced? Even there, because my workshop was under the bow, the exit went up through to the deck. It was a bit noisy down there and you could hear the shells coming out. It's a bit like a gun. When you fire the bullet, the shell comes out of the side. You'll have seen it in films. Well, these shell cases that came out from the turret were about four or five inches big.

"As soon as the firing was over, I used to get the lads who worked for me to open the hatch, bring down all these empty shell cases, and stack them in the workshop behind boxes and boxes of tiles. So, they were concealed, if there was an inspection or anything.

"When we came in to Hong Kong, there was a Chinese woman we knew called Jenny, who used to take in orphaned girls. Well, she was the main dealer. If you had anything to flog, you'd take it to Jenny. Any ship that went in to Hong Kong was always painted, right the way through, outside and in, this was on the consent of the Admiralty.

"So, we'd offered her these shell cases. Well, she didn't want them. We said we probably had about seventy of them. Then, she became interested. I had a friend who was a Petty Officer and Jenny suggested we do the deal on a particular lunchtime. So, she got her girls right the way through the main passage, all pretending to paint. They had canvas bags, which could take two shell cases at a time. So, the shells went in these bags, straight over the side into a Sampan (flat-bottomed Chinese wooden boat). Anyway, she cleared all the shells. I think I got about HK$16 per case, which was equivalent to about £2. I told Jenny that I could get some more for her and I went to the bloke who worked under the aft turret. It was dinner time and Charlie was eating, so I said my lads would move the shell cases for him, save interrupting his meal. So we moved all of his cases as well and, end of the day, I forget how much we made, but if we got HK$10 per case, we told Charlie would could only get HK$5 because the market had gone flat. So we made another few dollars that way.

"The other Chief Petty Officer and I split the profits in half – well, he got half of the profit from his side of the ship, he didn't get any of mine – and we went ashore that night to a nightclub in Hong Kong. We were having some drinks and I said to him, *'By the way, I reckon you owe me a few bob for hiding and moving all those shell cases. I think you owe me about HK$50. Unless you don't think you owe me. In which case, I might have to spill the beans...'* He laughed. He was quite happy with that. And my wife was happy as well because she ended up with a black pearl necklace, mounted on gold, and a black pearl ring, and she's still got both today.

"But I always laugh about that, when I got my good conduct medal because we always called it – *'Fifteen years of undetected crime'*.

"It was quite amusing because we were alongside the Andromeda in port and we sailed together for a time. My next-door neighbour from when I was a kid was serving on the Andromeda. In the end, we wound up in Hong Kong together. One of their chaps was electrocuted on board and we were due to go to a place called Phuket, pronounced Poo-kay.

"When I met up with my old neighbour in Hong Kong, they were inboard because they were the senior ship, and their leave had stopped twenty-four hours before ours. It was because theirs was a steamship. We used to get on the upper deck, and the voice would come on the Tannoy – *'Stand clear. Start the main engines.'* There'd be two puffs of exhaust, let go fore, let go aft, and we were gone. Incredibly fast but your clothes would stink of diesel, and the smell would never go.

"After being on a diesel ship for so long, my wife could always recognise the smell. So when we got back to Dartmouth, when someone opened the door to our pub, Barbara could always tell when there was a submarine out there because of this waft of diesel.

"When I was on the Dido, this young fella heard her say there was a submarine coming in, and he asked her how she knew.

"She said, *'I can smell them.'*

"*'I'm a submariner,'* the lad told her.

"*'My husband's in the Royal Navy,'* she said.

"*'And what do you do there?'* he asked.

"Well, we were anti-submarine crew, so I told him, *'Kill submariners.'*

"We were allowed to watch the missile going up. It was incredible the first time I saw it. The missile would go up about one hundred feet, level out and then – it was gone, you'd never see it again. We used to fire it at the ship's helicopter, which had passive sonar, so nothing else could pick it up. A submarine might have been just about able to pick us up, but we'd be miles away. So, having fired at the ship's helicopter, it would then take control of the missile. As it entered the water, it would do a 360° sweep. So, depending on where the submarine was when the missile entered the water, it might have been ten metres away, or a couple of hundred metres away. If it was a miss, you'd have two or three minutes to get away. But it was a dead cert. If we had fourteen missiles on board, that would be fourteen submarines hit.

"Actually, that was something. We worked for the Americans for a while. We went to Virginia and we showed the Americans how all this equipment worked, and one of them told their Chief that they'd have to order twenty of our frigates because they couldn't touch us. They couldn't believe it.

"There was a hurricane coming into Bermuda and our skipper said, *I'm sorry but this is the Royal Navy, we don't go in for wind.*'

"As it happened, we had to go in because of some problem and we spent the weekend in Bermuda. As we came out, within ten minutes, we'd picked up on this Russian submarine, and she was in range of the American coast. Of course, the Americans weren't too happy about that, but they still weren't convinced about our equipment.

"We followed it for six weeks and were able to radio the Americans and tell them exactly when the Russian sub was going to surface. We gave her longitude and latitude, and so, they flew over. As they did so, the Russian sub surfaced. But it was great equipment. If you were outside Plymouth, you could pick up a submarine on the Thames, and then just disappear.

"There was an author who wrote one of these spy-thriller books and, when I was reading it, I thought, *'This guy shouldn't be writing about all this. This is top secret!'*

"I don't remember the name of the book, but it goes to show, that saying – the walls have ears – is true, because he used to go down to Devonport, sit in the pub and just listen to the sailors, telling stories. If any of us had written it, we'd have been done under the Official Secrets Act.

"We had some close calls. There was one, on my last ship, Sirius. Coming out of Portland, we were only going out for a couple of days, but the night before, I was told to call my wife. It turned out, we weren't to know when we were coming back, and so I was allowed ashore to call Barbara.

"I said, *'We're sailing tomorrow.'* She knew that. I said, *'We don't know when we're coming back.'*

"She said, *'What do you mean?'*

"I said, *'I don't know.'*

"It was all top secret, so of course, I didn't know. Off we went, and the Captain came on and said, *'There's a Russian carrier coming up from the Mediterranean. We're going to go out and shadow it, find out where it's going.'*

"So we went down the Western Approaches, you see, and we got down to Penzance. Well, this Russian carrier turned round and started back down again. So we were allowed ashore. First thing, everyone got on the phone to their wives.

" *'Where are you?'* Barbara asked.

" *'Penzance,'* I said.

"Well, then this Russian carrier started coming back up again, and she kept on coming. We weren't really shadowing. We were about fifty yards off her stern, just plodding. The chopper was taking pictures but there was nothing happening. We were using the passive sonar, not like the old ASDICs – with their *ping-ping-ping* – we were in the dark, so they didn't know where we were, or that we were listening to her. We worked out that they must be going to an exercise somewhere. So, the idea came about that we should go active for a time, turn the ASDICs on. *Ping-ping-ping*. Well, that was it, you see. All hell broke loose and away she went.

"As we got up to the top of Scotland, someone else took over at Rosyth and we came all the way back. Of course, we thought we were going to go down to the Med, but it never happened.

"When I went out on Sirius, to Bermuda, that was the first time I'd ever been west.

"Every time I'd been out to sea, I always went east. We went out through the Suez Canal. On the Dido, we went to Syria and, as far as I know, we were the only warship to go to Syria since the Second World War. Of course, the Russians were there then, and they actually put a curfew on us – we weren't allowed to go ashore.

"We had some blokes who joined the ship at Gib, and they were in our mess. We called them the Secret Squirrels. They brought a lot of gear on board in what they called the Electronic Warfare Office. We didn't know what they were doing and then, one day, I asked one of them. He pointed to the mast and asked if I noticed anything different. I looked and, after a while, he pointed to this little box, about the size of a pint glass, with little balls on the top of it. He said, *'We fitted that.'* It was so small, and high up on the mast, you'd never have noticed it.

"It turned out, it was the most powerful aerial there was. And when we went into Latakia, which is a port in Syria, these guys went into the e-room and listened all night long. When we left – they had boxes and boxes of tapes – we went to Cyprus, where they were to be offloaded.

"Because they were sleeping in our mess – I should explain, they were up all night, so they would sleep during the day, of course we kept the lights down low – but one of these chaps was yapping away in his sleep, in Arabic. Well, his boss came in and shook him awake. Don't know what he was worried about – none of us could speak Arabic. Might as well have left him to chatter, we wouldn't have known what he was saying.

"After all this, we came back into Devonport. I was a Chief Petty Officer, but there was a job going at the Britannia Royal Naval College for a *Chief* Chief, if you like. So I was a Shipwright, First Class, which was a Chief, but up from that, you've got a Chief Shipwright. I'd gone for this at Fisgard but didn't pass. The only reason I took the exam was because of this job at the BRNC. It was suggested that I could take it again, but I wasn't worried about it, because I knew – if I passed it, I'd have been sent to Scotland.

"All the Devonport ships were small ships or frigates, which called for a Shipwright, First Class. But the Chief Shipwright might be sent to Portsmouth, for the missile ships, or to Scotland. Well, I didn't particularly want to go away from Devonport, and there wasn't a terrific amount of difference in pay, so I wasn't bothered about taking the exam again.

"A job came up at BRNC for a Chief Shipwright, and I was approached by the depot ship at the time – I was in charge of the depot ship itself, on the maintenance there – and I was sent for and told that there was this job at the Royal Naval College for an NBCDI, which I was qualified for. That's a Nuclear, Biological, Chemical Defence Instructor. They asked if I was interested and, of course, I was.

"They told me I'd have to go on a course on Phoenix, which was in Portsmouth. So, I did the course and I passed. In Portsmouth, it was quite amusing because it wasn't even a shipwright who took the course. It was a Chief Stoker. The first time we did an exercise – shoring up the space, stopping the water coming in, this Chief Stoker wasn't doing it properly. I asked him, *'Who on earth taught you?'*

"I said, *'Having been a shipwright for twenty years and an NBCDI for ten, I would never, ever do it that way.'*

"He told me I needn't bother coming to the next class. Which was fine with me. I still had to do the fire-fighting course, which annoyed me because I wouldn't be teaching fire-fighting at the College. I'd be on damage control and the nuclear side of things, the chemical side of things, but not fire-fighting. Anyway, we got through it and, when it came to the end, we were going to do a big exercise. He told me, *'You needn't bother coming in for that. I know you know what to do.'*

"So, I had the morning off and came in in the afternoon. It was then that Prince Harry was born. Now, the long tot had stopped in 1970-71, but with the birth of a grandchild, the Queen allowed us to 'splice the mainbrace'. I think I've told you before but a tot was a triple measure. As a senior rank, you were allowed to drink it neat. The ratings had grog, which was a treble measure of rum with two measures of water. You couldn't keep it like that, it would go like vinegar. But we, being the responsible ranks, were allowed to drink it neat.

"So, this was the afternoon that I was coming in, having had the morning off. I was in Victory Barracks, and a bloke came in and reminded me that I hadn't had my tot. I said I'd have what was called 'mismusters', because I had to drive to Portsmouth, to spend the afternoon on this course, but I'd come back. He told me there were no mismusters. I'd have to have it there and then, or not have it at all. So, I had my tot then, with a pint of beer. And then, I went on to Phoenix.

"*'Ah, Chippy, I've got your tot here,'* a voice said.

"I said, *'I've just had it at Victory.'*

"*'Well, they don't know that,'* he replied.

"So, I had another one, and another beer. Needless to say, we didn't do the rest of the course.

"One of the blokes was on a ship in the dockyard and he asked me if I had my car. I'd had two tots, two beers, and he said, *'Well, you can drive them down.'* So I drove everybody down to the dockyard, went on board... Had another pint, and then, I drove back. But that was the last time I had a tot – in 1984.

"And then, I was at the College and quite enjoyed it. One story from there is the time that I buggered my back up again. They put me into traction. They weren't sure if they were going to operate or what. There was a lot of pain. After a while, it settled down. There was a female doctor there, a lieutenant.

"Anyway, I was teaching at BRNC and one of the classes I took was for doctors and dentists. In one of the classes, all these doctors and dentists were issued gas masks and then, they went into the gas chamber, because they'd been given a quick briefing on nuclear and biological warfare. There were about twenty of these doctors and dentists, so I welcomed them to the class, and I explained that I appreciated their time for this very important lesson. And, as I was looking around, I saw this woman.

"I said, *'I know you from somewhere.'*

" '*No, no,*' she said.

"So, I turned round to write something on the chalkboard and I suddenly stopped and turned back. I said, '*I do know you.*' She went bright red. I said, '*You were the junior doctor on my ward, a few months ago, when I was in for my back.*' I said, '*Guess what... It's my turn today.*'"

<Lots of laughter>

"So we went down to the gas chamber. It was right down by the river, and I used to get them to wear the suits and the masks and then go at the double around this field. I'd just stroll down there. Well, with all the gear on, by the time they got to me, they were sweating and tired, but it showed them what it was like to actually wear the stuff.

"So then we get to the gas chamber. The chamber was full of CS gas and I told them that, when we got in, I would point to one of them. That person would then remove their mask, tell me their name, and walk out. I reminded them not to rub their eyes and made sure they all understood.

"So, it came time to point to this junior doctor. I pointed at her. She took off her gas mask. Told me her name and went to walk out.

"I took hold of her arm and said, '*Excuse me? I didn't hear that.*'

"She tried again. Her eyes were streaming. I said, '*I told you it was my turn.*'"

Peter

"ALL MY SERVICE LIFE has been in the police force. I joined the Worcestershire Constabulary as a cadet in 1962. I did two years as a cadet, which was different to what a cadet is now. This was an employed position with training to become a police officer. On reaching the grand age of nineteen, I became eligible to become a Constable.

"Then, Worcestershire and a lot of police forces had height conditions because you were supposed to rise above the crowd of course. Worcestershire had their height set at 5'10". I was 5'9". I was told to stick some horse manure in my shoes to try and make 5'10". I got to 5'9¼" and they had this great deliberation about whether or not to appoint me as a Constable but decided that I was worth having and I was duly appointed an officer of the Crown. Nothing like a PCSO who is not an officer at all! Constables were modelled on the military with similar uniforms and subject to similar discipline but there was a particular difference. Constables acted under their own right in law and not under orders to execute their duty – although many preferred to be told what to do. Ranks in the police did not change the status of constable. No ranked constable could tell me who to arrest or not. They could of course tell me what, where, how and when to work.

"An important responsibility was exercising discretion about arrest, prosecution, warning or advice. Police were the prosecution authority – no CPS then. We prosecuted only if there was a case to answer and it mattered not if a defendant was found not guilty.

"I went off on a three-month training course in Ryton-on-Dunsmore. Out of all the recruits from all over the Midlands, I came out with the Baton of Honour, which was quite an achievement.

"I returned to my force. I had to do two years' probationary service, which you probably still do but it will have changed. You had to do that on the beat. I was posted to Evesham, where I became known as Golden Bollocks."

<Me: Fabulous.>

"Yes, this was because my approach to policing was – if you deal with the small things, every now and again, you'll get a big thing. Most of my colleagues, even then in the 60s, avoided the small things because they were keeping themselves back for the big things. Now that is the standard. Prevention is out of the window and so is dealing with so-called minor offences – unless it is exceeding an appropriate speed limit without any element of danger.

"So, I would deal with people for all sorts of relatively minor offences. My feeling was that people who would commit minor offences were more likely to commit the more serious offences.

"We were, at that time, responsible for prosecution and decisions about going to court. This is before the Crown Prosecution Service, which is – pathetic, really, but there it is. The point is: I was dealing with the small things and looking deeper to see if there was anything more serious behind it. And my arrest rate increased much more than that of my colleagues. It was just a case of being persistent.

"For example: I stopped a guy in a flash sports car with a number plate that had been doctored. I said, *'That's not quite right.'* His response was sufficient to make me go through the whole routine – asking for his driving licence, insurance, all that sort of thing. And then, I checked the engine. It was a stolen car. Just from the number plate being altered a little bit... He was a spivvy type of character.

"Then you'd get people who were parked in the wrong place. And they'd ask: *'Are you on the square?'*

"So, I'd say, *'No, I'm not.'*

"The guy would come back with, *'Well, I know your Chief Constable.'*

"I'd say, *'Well, so do I.'"*

<Laughter>

"I'd say, *'Do you want me to tell him that you tried to avoid action by introducing his name?'*

"See, you could deal with things like that, not necessarily by taking them to court, but you could win – by talking.

"Anyway, Evesham was a place, rather like the Garden of Eden – but in England, a bit like Kent, with a lot of apples and pears, plums, a lot of fruit in the area, and so, by extension, a lot of seasonal workers who tended to be travellers. And they were fine. Really, they were essential.

"Every Friday and Saturday night, the pubs in the town would explode. Which was – fair enough. We, the single men among the officers – who were mostly men, although there were some ladies – would deal with it if these guys decided to kick off in the pubs. But those of us who lived above the station would be in the Police Club (most of which have been disbanded now) and wait for the shout.

"We were off-duty and there would be a call for assistance. We'd jump into our own cars, after a few pints – it was a different time – we'd race up the High Street, we'd sort out all these characters, lock them up for the night and then, we'd go back and have another few pints. And that was kind of a routine. There wasn't any paid overtime. It was all part of the job. Perhaps that's been forgotten.

"There was a particular incident at Evesham, one of many. I was on early turn. On shift work, we worked on the half-hour, so it went 1.30-9.30, 9.30-5.30, 5.30-1.30. It was pretty tough. I don't think they do that now, but every three shifts we had what was called a 'quick turnover'. So, we'd finish at half-nine in the evening and then had to be back, fully fit for duty at half-five the following morning, but they also required us to parade fifteen minutes earlier. So, we had to be on parade at 5.15am having finished – if indeed we did finish on time – at 9.30 the night before.

"Even on those occasions, we would go off to a local pub where we could – refresh. We'd come back, sometimes with no sleep, and get ready for the parade. I think, on this occasion, I hadn't had much sleep but at 5.15, I paraded for duty. It was winter. I had a British Warm overcoat, which service people would know, which went over the standard uniform – none of this t-shirt nonsense – and I'd gone out for early morning patrol. We didn't usually get much activity in the early morning.

"So, I walked around the streets and out jumps an Irishman. He stood in front of me and said, *'Come on, then.'*

"I was rather bleary at that time of day, but he tried again. *'Come on, come on! Put 'em up. I want to fight you.'*

"*'At half past five in the morning?'* I asked.

"And he started on me. I mean, I'm not a fighter but we wound up rolling round and round on a concrete path. I can see it now. I got on top of him, sweating buckets in this overcoat and I took his head in my hands and banged it on the pavement.

"*'Okay, okay, you win,'* he said.

"*'All right,'* I said. *'So long as you promise to behave.'*

"He called me a cowboy but we shook hands, and then I arrested him. So, I took him to the station and locked him up. The sergeant asked why I'd arrested him, so I explained that he'd attacked me and we'd had this fight, so I'd arrested him for being drunk and disorderly.

"*'At half past five in the morning?'* he asked.

"There was a rule, actually, set by the sergeant not to arrest people for drunkenness because they were usually on the cider and it would stink out the cells. So we were under pressure not to arrest people for drunkenness, only if they were disorderly or violent, but not if they were just drunk.

"So, in those days, you'd bring them up immediately at the next court session – that same morning. So, I went into court and the magistrate was there and this guy I'd arrested said, *'Yes, I admit it, your worships. He's a cowboy but I've learnt my lesson.'*

"I had no further trouble in Evesham from that day. Generally speaking, Evesham was a very peaceful, ordinary town and we had great fun.

"Whilst at Evesham, the routine was that there would be three or four of us on duty on nights. Usually three, sometimes two, but one would be in charge of the station, which had to be manned at all times. One of the jobs of the station officer was to keep the boiler going, stoking it up and all the rest of it, and looking after any prisoners. They'd also have to do filing of paperwork, including the Police Gazette.

"So, I was sat there, just twiddling my thumbs. I had two PCs out on the streets and the Sergeant had told me before he went off that, at two o'clock, I was to release the guy in custody. I can't remember what he'd been arrested for – drinking, possibly. Anyway, two o'clock in the morning, I was to throw him out. I was stoking the fire, all was peaceful in the town, and I was getting this prisoner ready for release. I told him, *'You can go now.'*

"Off he goes, and I went about filing the paperwork. I was going through the Police Gazettes and this picture jumped out at me. It was the chap I'd just released. Wanted for murder in Bolton, Lancashire. At that time, it was a different force. So, I thought, *'Bloody hell, what do I do now?'*

"What I shouldn't have done was lock up the police station and go and look for him, but that's what I did. Now, near to the police station was a bus park and it was well-known to us because the drivers would leave the buses unlocked and it was a great place to go off and have a little kip. So, I went up to this bus, opened the door and there was this guy, asleep on the back seat.

"I said, *'I'm glad I found you. I'm in a bit of a bind because I've released you without completing all the paperwork. Could you come back and we'll get it all signed off?'*

"So, he agreed. We got back to the police station and I arrested him for murder. I wound up getting a commendation for that – it sounds like a feather in your cap to arrest someone for murder, doesn't it? But really, it was a mixture of accident and luck, I suppose.

"Jumping ahead. I was transferred to Birmingham, to the Midland Criminal Record Office. In there, we used to publish the Midland Criminal Record Information Sheet, which was about local people who were wanted for various crimes. It was like the Police Gazette but local. I also had to deal with what was then Identikit. I would go and interview victims of crime and get descriptions of the perpetrators, and I would create Identikit composite pictures. Then, I would have to go through all our records to try and sort out who might fit the description and the type of offence. So, I did quite a lot of those, including murderers, and it was very successful.

"Whilst I was in the Midland Criminal Record Office, I also had to prepare the scripts for *Shaw Taylor's Police 5* – it was a regular five minute police programme which would explain about particular offences and appeal for witnesses. Shaw Taylor was a Midlands TV guy and I would give him the script and discuss it.

"During my two year secondment in Birmingham, I married my wife, who was a policewoman. It was rather uncanny because we'd both been on patrol in Evesham and wherever I went on my beat, she would appear."

<Me: Was she stalking you?>

"Not stalking precisely... Anyway, she won. So, we got married in Halesowen, which is part of the Black Country. As a policewoman, she didn't work full nights because they were a protected species then, but they only got paid 90% of what a PC got.

"Now, if she was on-call, I'd be in bed and very often, during the early hours, there would be banging on the bedroom windows and stones being thrown against the glass – communication then wasn't quite what it is now – but you'd wake up to this rattling noise and flashes of light across the bedroom, and it was always for my wife. There would be a couple of PCs outside, who'd been sent to get her to go and deal with a woman prisoner. This was quite common. Off she'd go, and I'd go back to sleep again.

"It's peculiar when you think of it now, when everyone has mobile phones, but it was – part of the history of real policing, I suppose.

"After my secondment, they had already appointed me as a Detective Constable. Now, because there'd been an amalgamation with West Mercia while I was on secondment, they'd changed the rules. So having been appointed a Detective Constable, they appointed me as an Aide to CID for three months at Stourbridge.

"At the end of the three months' aideship, I was considered unsuitable to be a detective and was told to take a residential beat in Cradley village, deep in the Black Country. The previous two PCs had retired on sick leave. So, I didn't fancy it. I was told that it was just right for me, that I'd soon sort it out. And I said I was going to apply to transfer to another force.

"The Assistant Chief Constable called me in and said that they didn't want to lose me. He thought I'd probably prefer to be a village Bobby. As it turned out, there were several vacancies in the force area, so he suggested I go around them, with my wife, and pick which one I wanted-ed. So, I did and I picked the village of West Hagley, which is in between Stourbridge and Kidderminster but it was in the same Division.

"I had this village police station. I settled into the area, and I was told I was on a par with the local vicar. It was an interesting place because it was like this village – rather upmarket and it was thought to be a very law-abiding place without much really going on.

"Well, all that changed with me. I didn't cause the crime, you under-stand, I was just clearing it up. I used to patrol on my BSA motorbike, which was a noisy bloody thing. So, I would go out on this motorbike and, particularly in the evenings, when the kids were gathered in the village centre, they'd hear me coming. But they all knew who I was and we didn't have a lot of trouble there.

"What we did have were invasions from the Greater Birmingham area, especially when there were dances. In the village hall, I was called in to deal with some trouble. I ended up having tables and chairs wrapped round my head; I was knocked unconscious by this gang. The call went out and all the reinforcements came charging out from Stourbridge. And these poor teenagers, I felt terribly sorry about this, in all the com-motion, parents had come to collect their kids and they ended up being arrested because they were standing around. So, they were being thrown into police vans and I was being taken off to hospital.

"The Chief Superintendent and the Superintendent went to tell my wife that I was in hospital. Her story is, she was disturbed by this knock on the door at one or two o'clock in the morning. When she looked out of the window, she saw two men, and decided not to answer the door. So they gave up. She only found out where I'd been at around six in the morning, when I was released from the hospital.

"It transpired, only a couple of months after that, the leader of this gang was arrested for murder. So, that felt a bit close.

"Another time, I had to deal with some kids who'd broken into a railway hut and stolen some warning caps, for fun. So, I found out who it was but what I didn't realise was that it was a really serious offence – Obstruction of a railway or trains – and it had to be tried by the Quarter Session, which was one step down from the Assize court where the red robed judges sat and put on a black cap if a murderer was to be hanged. Fortunately that didn't happen to the kids who were convicted.

"There were two memorable events. There was a care-home on my patch, for girl offenders. They were always running away and I had to go out and find them. There was one occasion when two girls ran off. I was told they were running over a field, so I shouted to them that I was going to have to release the dog. I didn't have a dog but they didn't know that. And they stopped and I was able to take them back.

"But I was particularly keen to watch out for burglary. On this one occasion, I was on the motorbike and I saw a van that looked a bit suspicious, because it was travelling slowly in an area of high-value housing. So, I stopped and checked them, found out who they were, driving licence details and all that sort of thing. By that time, we had these two-way radios – one receiver and one transmitter. So, I got this call – *'The officer checking so-and-so and so-and-so, clear off!'*

"It transpired, and I was most annoyed about this, that the Crime Squad was setting up the driver of this van and detectives were stationed all around me, hiding in the ditches. I was fuming. The house they were going to burgle was on my patch. So were they. Because I'd ruined their set-up, it didn't do me much good as a prospective detective. I was just a good PC. Further damage resulted in my insistence in recording a burglary as a burglary. The Detective Inspector told me to mark it down as a theft to save the statistics. I refused, so he said I had better detect it so I did.

"We used to have a regular system of looking after people's houses while they were away on holiday. So, I'd check it, walk around the side of the property, all the way around and look at the doors and windows and such. One particular time, there was a house that was void, as we called it.

"I was on patrol and I saw this car parked some way away from it, on the verge. So I had a look at it, nobody in it, but it was parked quite close to this house. So, I checked the house, everything seemed to be in order. I was suspicious and went up the road and parked in a little lay-by for a few minutes. I watched as the Detective Chief Inspector drove past. Then, this suspect car comes along. On with the blue light, and he stopped.

"He asked me why I'd pulled him over and so I told him that I'd seen his car parked up the road, on the verge there. He told me he'd just been visiting relatives. So, I asked him to open the back of his car. Eventually, he did and there were three pillowcases full of silverware and goodness' knows what. I asked him what it all was and he made something up – his auntie was moving or something similar – well, I didn't fall for it and I arrested him. I got a commendation for that, but I enjoyed pointing out to the Detective Chief Inspector that he had driven past this car and done nothing about it.

"So, my time as a village beat officer was really quite active but it was twenty-four hour responsibility and, of course, it occupied your house and everywhere you were.

"As a village Bobby, you inevitably have a lot of dealings with families, you could deal with kids who'd done a bit of shoplifting, without going all the way to Court, and all the rest of it. You could talk to them, you could caution them, you'd have the family there, all of it, without making a record. You weren't *not* doing your job, that was part of it – because what I'm really talking about here is prevention of crime. The right word, at the right time. That was a valuable part of policing and I think it was appreciated.

"Then, I got promoted to Sergeant. I was called in to headquarters and the Assistant Chief Constable said, *'I want you to start something new. We're going to do accident investigation, using maths and science and all that sort of stuff and we reckon that you can do that.'*

"I did have a GCE in maths but I wouldn't consider myself, at any time, a mathematician. Or, indeed, a scientist.

"But no, he said, *'We're going to set this unit up and you'll have a colleague Sergeant as well, and the two of you will deal with fatal road accidents.'*

"So we started all this stuff – which is fairly commonplace now, although we never allowed a road to be closed off for hours, as they do now – but we would rush out to the scene of a serious accident and we'd work it all out, draw up scale plans and use the formula for working out speed from skid marks – and we'd do a reconstruction. And it wasn't always what you would expect. Sometimes, we'd be able to prove that somebody who might have been accused and, indeed, convicted, was not at fault. If they'd come out from a Give Way sign and there was a car on the major road, and a collision, it was normally assumed that the car at the Give Way sign had failed to give way and was therefore, at fault. However, with our calculations, we were able to prove, for example, that when the car emerged from the Give Way sign, the car on the major road would not have been in sight. And if the car on the major road was going at high speed, the driver at the Give Way sign might not have had a chance to avoid him. It was fascinating.

"I was asked to go on a working party to set up a national scheme for accident investigation, so I did that. That was enjoyable. As a Traffic Sergeant and accident investigator, I sometimes had to stand in the control room to supervise it. On this one occasion, I was doing that, and a tanker overturned on the M5. The Patrol Sergeant said, *I'm worried about the contents of this tanker, which appears to be leaking – we could have a serious explosion.'*

"So, we had to close the motorway, which hadn't really been done before anywhere else, and it caused chaos. None of the diversions were geared up for it. It just log-jammed the whole place. As it turned out, it was only diesel from the cab and not the flammable contents of the tank, so we got through that. But – they didn't let me go into the control room anymore."

<Laughter>

"Nevertheless, I went up for promotion on two or three occasions, and the horrible Chief Constable that we had then – he's dead now – but when it came to going up before the promotion boards, he'd ask, *'Have you got rid of that chip off your shoulder yet?'*"

<Me: I dislike him intensely already.>

"I told him I didn't have a chip on my shoulder. He replied, *'Oh, yes you have. I can still see it. Come back next year.'*

"So, when I went before the board for the third time, he asked, *'Have you got rid of that chip off your shoulder yet?'* and I said, *'Oh, yes, thank you, I have.'*

" *'Good,'* he said, and promoted me to Inspector. It really was stupid. So then, he called me up and told me he was sending me up to Shrewsbury to live in this particular police house, and to sell my own house in Droitwich. He finished by telling me that I was to move on 23rd December.

"I had two children in school and asked for more time.

"He asked, *'Is there a problem?'*

"I explained that the proposed date of the move was two days before Christmas, it would mean going a distance of seventy miles or so, and with two children, it was a bit...

" *'No problem,'* he said. *'We'll sort out the removal. But I want you there before Christmas.'* There was a pause. Then finally, he said, *'I can tell you're a bit doubtful so, to clarify – if you don't take it, you won't be promoted.'*

"So, that was it. We went to Shrewsbury, two days before Christmas and when we got there – the house had been empty for a long time, the boiler didn't work. It was all rather chaotic but we got through it.

"There was a time – I got a call that there was a man on the roof of Shrewsbury Prison. It took some weighing up because anything might be wrong with him, he might be suffering or... And he was dressed as Father Christmas. He had a sack and he was throwing things from this sack into the prison yard.

"So, we were confronted by this scene, and then we found out that ITV were racing out from Birmingham. He'd done it as some sort of publicity stunt. The fact was, we needed a ladder to get him down. We would have got ladders from the fire brigade, but they were on strike.

"Green Goddess came trundling up, with a couple of guys and a Second Lieutenant. So, he saluted and, *'What do you need us to do, sir?'*

"So I asked him to get the ladder in place and send someone up to go and collect this chap.

"*'I can put the ladder up for you, sir,'* he said, *'but I can't send anyone to get him because we're not insured for that.'* The British Army, not insured?

"With that, I wound up climbing up the ladder. All the way to the top, I'm not very good on heights, but I spoke to this man. Well, he only wanted to know if ITV was there yet! I told him they weren't coming, that they'd been told to stand down. He was disappointed but I got him to come down the ladder and I arrested him, and took him back to the station.

"Because it was a major incident, the Chief Super was called in. I told him I'd arrested this chap. He wondered what for. So, I said, *'Vagrancy Act 1824, sir,'* because he'd been found in enclosed premises for an unlawful purpose. The unlawful purpose was – he'd been throwing cigarettes out of the sack to the prisoners. And he got six months.

"Twelve months after this, I'd been on an Inspector's course at the police college. I was already a Detective Inspector – which righted previous wrongs and amused me. I'd been away on this course for three months, and we had a little gathering of detectives when I came back. I asked what had been happening since I'd been away.

"Well, it turned out there had been a big scare in Shrewsbury, which had caused a lot of problems, because someone sent a bomb to the prison. It was, in fact, a hoax, but they hadn't known that when it appeared – it basically closed Shrewsbury down. It was a shoebox in brown paper packaging, and inside was an alarm clock, wires and candles.

"Forensics hadn't found anything on the packaging, or on the clock or the wires. So, I said, *'What about this, then?'*

"There was a white envelope, sealed, that nobody had noticed. So they all felt rather silly, but this envelope was addressed to the prison governor. Inside the envelope was a card, which read, *'To the governor of HMP Shrewsbury, this is to frighten the living daylights out of you.'* And we read the signature and, lo and behold, it was the guy who'd been on the prison roof as Father Christmas.

"In fact, he'd made a bit of a name for himself with his publicity stunts. At one point, he'd nailed himself to a tree (well, he'd got someone to help him with that). He'd swallowed some frogs another time, and he was actually a very intelligent guy. He had quite a scientific background. Anyway, we went to look for him and we found him in a café.

"Well, he knew he recognised me.

" *'RAF?'* he asked.

" *'No,'* I said, and reminded him about the incident on the prison roof. Then, he realised that we'd come about the bomb. So, he was arrested for that, and he did another six months.

"While I was at the police college, I was told I was being put forward to do a university degree. In those days, police officers with university degrees were very, very rare. So, it was quite something to be recommended for this, but it was up to me to get a place at a university. I applied to several universities, including Exeter, and I got offers from all of them, including Oxford.

"So, I went to St John's College, Oxford, to read Human Sciences, which was all about people, evolution, genetics, anthropology, behaviour, health and ecology. During those three years, I developed a concept of what I called 'ecological policing'. It was to do with the way ecology affects behaviour. The idea was, if you could deal with environmental issues as part of policing, and incorporate the nutritional and behavioural health of offenders, you could see what made them offend and look to preventing further instances of offence.

"I was awarded a grant from the Airey Neave Memorial Trust to further my studies, and I went out to America, Canada, West Indies and Hong Kong. It furthered my interest in the nutritional condition of a person and how it affected behaviour.

"Of course, when I returned to policing, I was considered an academic, not a proper policeman. So the horrible Chief Constable told me, *'You've been away for three years, you went away against my advice, and you'll have to serve your punishment. It'll be another three years before I consider you for promotion.'* As far as he was concerned, I'd had a holiday.

"Anyway, during my time in the States, I'd been to an American police station to interview the Chief. As I came out – I turned left. The road wasn't busy, and I could or should have stopped, but I saw a gap in the oncoming traffic and I zipped across – right in front of a patrol car.

"Suddenly, the lights were flashing, and they pulled me over. The Officer got his gun out as I explained that I'd made an error and I was sorry. He swore at me, and he rattled on about how terrible my driving was, and he then realised I was British. In Britain, we do stupid things like driving on the left.

"*'When are you leaving the country?'* he asked.

"*'Tomorrow, actually,'* I said.

" *'Good,'* he said. *'Don't come back.'*

"So, I came back to this country, and was put back into uniform as an Inspector, out of CID again. One funny thing that happened – we had a call to say there was a burglary in progress on the outskirts of Kidderminster, way out in the country. So, we went off to that. I picked up one of the burglars and was bringing him back to the station. He was in the backseat. It was a very wet, rainy night. There was a lot of mud on the roads, and we came up to this great big bend. I thought, *'I'm not going to get round this.'*

"I could see there was a five-bar gate straight ahead and, although I wanted to turn right, it was just too wet and muddy, we'd never have made it. So, I hit the brakes – skidding like mad – and stopped just short of the gate.

"And you know what this guy said? *'If you think I'm going to cough out of that... You're not scaring me, you know.'* 'Cough' was slang for confession. There was a significant cough to come.

"I was continuing to have a rather interesting police life. Then, there started to be an increase in forces advertising for appointments. Particularly for Superintendent and Chief Inspector. Because I was still in purgatory, I applied for a Chief Inspector job in Humberside. I got it, and said goodbye to West Mercia.

"Humberside was different. I was already carrying the ignominious label of being an academic, so I was getting all sorts of research jobs. But I immediately fell foul of the Detective Superintendent who had been applying for the monthly expenses and exaggerating them. That caused a big problem because it landed me with another label: they said I was anti-CID, which was completely untrue. As a Detective Inspector, you really can't be anti-CID. So I wasn't all that happy in Humberside.

"Well, then West Yorkshire advertised for a Superintendent, so I went for that and got it. So, I was now an academic in West Yorkshire. There were some interesting episodes there. For example: there was this movement to establish victim suites, particularly for cases of abuse. So, I advised what they should do in setting up a suite for children, in particular, who might be reluctant to speak about crimes they'd be subjected to.

"The interview room, I told them, should be sky blue. All manner of people from social services insisted it should be green and it turned into a bit of a back-and-forth about what colour it should be, but I had the last word. Blue it was.

"Because we filmed the interviews, I could see what the children were reacting to in the room. So, we had these large flip-charts of coloured paper, and the kids would draw on them and flip the pages. As the colours became – more reds and yellows than anything else – they would speed up, do a scribble and flip again, getting stressed. So, I said we should have plain paper and pens. And it really made a difference and this particular blue had a calming effect.

"I set up an experiment in the police cells in Huddersfield. The police cells then were manned by old coppers – who were reliable, if a bit staid. In Huddersfield, I painted one cell a particular shade of pink. It was shocking pink. So, I had them put one offender in the pink cell and the next offender would go in the standard magnolia cell. And they thought it was a load of rubbish.

"This one particular character was always being arrested for drunk and disorderly, and was violent. When in police custody, he was known to kick off, shouting and banging, causing damage to the cell, that sort of thing. The custody officer said that he would prove the experiment wrong and put him in the pink cell.

"So, in he went. And he was quiet within minutes. The custody officers went to the cell and looked through the spy-hole and they saw him on his bed, kneeling and singing quietly. It was a hymn. This was within ten minutes of his being in the cell. It was an incredible result and convinced the custody staff. The problem was it went national. It wound up being used in prisons and police stations all over the place but they used different shades of pink and it did not work so well. It is the energy wavelength of light which we see as colours that affected the physiological and psychological condition.

"Then I moved on to nutrition. We did trials which were published and still stand. I got together ten youngsters who were always in trouble. In actual fact, there were eight but when I went to the parents, a couple of younger brothers were sent along too. It was interesting because the parents knew when their child was in trouble, or going to be in trouble.

"They'd say, *'Well, he's going to be a criminal...'*

"We had specialist doctors and we assessed each one, as to their nutritional condition. There were analyses, hair, blood, etc. So we got a good picture of how they were, in terms of their physical health. We also had them assessed via the scales that were then used for Asperger's and the autistic spectrum. Most of them were on the spectrum. Some of them were on Ritalin, which disturbs nutrition. Some of them had been excluded from school. Most had committed offences: burglary, theft, drugs, violence, using knives, threatening behaviour, and similar. There was one girl – who happened to be the worst of the lot.

"We had to take them from West Yorkshire to a particular surgical laboratory in London. We took them down on this bus. It was an awful journey. They were throwing things around, magazines and bits of paper, all over the bus and out of the window, littering. It was mayhem and this girl was dominating and winding up the rest of them.

"After we got them to the surgery, this girl flew past me to attack a lad, and I gave her a smack. And she stopped. She turned. She looked at me and she said, *'You've just hit me. You're not allowed to do that.'* Which was quite true, but I told her she wasn't allowed to attack the other kids either. She stopped.

"When I got them all home, I went to see her parents and I told them what had happened. *'Good for you!'* they said. That probably wouldn't happen now.

"Anyway, the trials were very successful. We showed we could identify their allergies and dietary intolerances, we'd identified their mineral deficiencies, and we'd changed their diets and, at the end of it, most of them were fine. Some reverted because of peer pressure, but most were happy and healthy by the end of it. Now, this girl had a big turn-around. She stopped offending. Completely. Wonderful. Later, she became a prostitute.

"Some time later, I got a call – this was not long after the Hungerford case – there was a guy with a shotgun, going around, threatening to shoot people, in Bradford. The firearms team was dealing with it and I drove twenty miles to get there. By the time I did, this guy had been arrested. I was told he was drunk, he'd had a few cans of beer on him, so he was drunk. So, I went to talk to him.

"I said, *'Were you drunk?'*

"He said, *'No.'* His solicitor agreed.

"Neither of us thought he was drunk, so I got a blood sample and a hair sample and sent them off to be analysed. When the results came back, they showed that he was over the driving limit, that he had mineral deficiencies, and excessive levels of copper and cadmium in his system. Now, copper is an essential mineral but it has a proven effect on mental health. Eventually, he went to court and the Detective Chief Inspector complained to the Chief Constable about me interfering. The Chief Constable told me to stop meddling and using tests which were too expensive.

"So, I told him we'd done the standard driving blood analysis. And the other analysis, I'd got done for nothing. Well, he told me not to do it again and shouted at me. And then he moved me on, to sort out problems with the communications. At that time, they had five different communications rooms.

"*'Why do you want me to do that?'* I asked.

"*'I just – think it's something you can do,'* he said.

"Well, I had no experience in communications whatsoever. So, I retired. We came down to Exeter and I continued to pursue my studies, having achieved my MPhil in Complementary Medicine.

"I did some further studies. I went to Winchester Barracks and to Lympstone. I got together twenty young soldiers, either recruits or in their early service, and I compared them with twenty prisoners in a Young Offenders' Institution in Portland. I did the various blood tests, hair tests, assessments and so forth, and I was able to show that the soldier group was much better nutritionally that the prisoner group – which you would expect. However, three of the twenty soldiers were discharged, or about to be discharged, because they didn't come up to standards. And they were the three highest scoring on my tests.

"So, I had this discussion with the Colonel and we talked about my tests and how they might help with recruiting and retention in the Army. Because, if you ran these tests whilst they were in training, you could correct their diets and assist their overall development.

"His response was, *'Well, that's all very interesting but we couldn't do that. On the battlefield, we can't get them special diets.'*

"But I wasn't talking about the battlefield, of course, I was talking about training. That said, they'd surely be better off in the battlefield if they'd had all this stuff sorted out beforehand.

"On the prisoner side of it, again there were interesting results, but they wouldn't be getting special diets either. Even though, they would get special diets if they happened to be vegetarian. They would get a special diet if they had to have it for religious reasons. So, I asked why they couldn't have a special diet based on these tests.

"*'Oh, can't have that. That's putting them in charge,'* I was told.

"Anyway, even though I moved into a more academic environment, and studied nutrition and the ecology of policing, my approach has always been about – doing myself out of a job."

<Me: I like that. What a great attitude.>

"The general objective within police work is the prevention of crime, but if you can prevent criminality, why wouldn't you?"

About the Author

Petrina Binney is from 1980s south London. Daughter of a nurse and a carpenter, she spent much of her childhood writing stories to bring into school for whatever the eighties English equivalent of 'Show and Tell' was called. She spent her teenage years avoiding all manner of naughtiness, instead writing copious amounts of self-indulgent poetry and reading multiple Brontës and Daphne Du Maurier. Since late in 2017, Petrina has written and published several volumes of the Sex, Death and Dinner series, and learnt to speak about herself in the third person. Petrina spends the majority of her time in Devon, with her dogs, drinking with older gentlemen and awaiting international notoriety. Read more at https://www.facebook.com/PetrinaAuthor/

Printed in Poland
by Amazon Fulfillment
Poland Sp. z o.o., Wrocław

50147409R00108